Wealth Maker

Or

Wishful Thinker

Getting From Where You Are To Where You Want To Be

Iustin Rosioara

Wealth Maker or Wishful Thinker:

Getting From Where You Are To Where You Want To Be

Copyright: Iustin Rosioara, 2015
www.MasteringTheHumanExperience.com

Images & EBook Cover Design: Wanda Rosioara
Book Cover Design: Andrei Dan (*andreidan43@yahoo.com*)
Author photo: Alex Kruyer (*www.alexkruyerphotography.com*)

EBook ISBN: 978-0-9961628-0-7

Paperback ISBN: 978-0-9961628-1-4

Published in the USA by Service Strategy Solutions, LLC, Minnesota

Table of Contents

Acknowledgments

This book is a result of many inputs. As difficult as it is to include everyone to whom I am grateful, I will give it a try. In order to be fair, I have to say that there were people who helped me in different ways—and whom I disappointed. Their names do not appear here because I preferred to contact them personally.

Before anything else, I thank God for giving me the wisdom and insight as well as the resources, guidance, and desire to put these concepts into writing.

I would like to thank my pastor, Randy Morrison of Speak the Word Church International, and also the late Dr. Myles Munroe of Bahamas Faith Ministries International. Their materials were invaluable in the process of understanding my own place in the world and the call upon my life; their messages brought much-needed common-sense understanding about topics that come up when we discuss failure and its root causes—identity, significance, bondage of the past, fighting deception, and so many others—that helped me in putting my life back on track. Listening to and processing all these messages allowed me to build a strong foundation for my future, especially in the way they made me receptive to the support from the people mentioned below. Without this foundation, their help would have had a minor impact in my life, or none at all.

I am so grateful for the support of my closest family members, including my mother, Maria, and my sister Magdalena (and her husband, Valenti), who have been very patient and believed in me even in times when there seemed to be no hope.

I am thankful to my dear cousin Valentina who, together with my aunt Anastasia; her husband, Dorian; and their daughter Laura, were there for me at a time when I had no clue where life was supposed to take me. Their support was priceless.

Among my friends, I would like to thank Petre Godeanu and Marc Cannizo. Throughout those years, both always made themselves available whenever I called them, and they have always encouraged me to move ahead. I also owe a lot to Sorin Costea and Børre Haukeboe - great helpers in two very tough moments of my life.

I am so grateful to Ela Dinca, who showed me what it means to offer so much without asking anything in return; and to Cristina Simionescu, who, despite the fact that I proved to be such a disappointment, kept threatening to kill me for not believing in myself.

A special person in my life is Svein Grødum, who was simultaneously a mentor, a boss, a business partner, and a friend. Over the years, I learned that his trusting in me meant much more than I was aware of when we working together.

I am thankful to John Tschohl, the president of Service Quality Institute, and his wife, Patricia, who gave me the chance to spend over a year in the United States, making it possible to meet the wonderful woman who is now my wife.

I am also grateful to Barb Valencour, who always helped me to focus on my strengths and encouraged me to live out my destiny.

A special thank you goes to Lauri Flaquer for all the wonderful meetings and chats and all her ideas and insights that made this book possible. I am also grateful for the support of my editor, Lynn Cross, for all the work done to make this book publishable.

Finally, I want to thank my children, of whom I am so proud: Ana Maria, an IT entrepreneur, for all her patience in providing technology support to a technologically deficient father; and my son, Christian, who proved, at the age of only 21, to have much more maturity than I ever showed, even at the age of 40.

Last (but not least) is my wife, Wanda—the amazing woman who chose to believe in me not only as a friend, but as a partner for life. It's hard for me to find words to describe how much she means to me. For sure, she is the one who made me believe again in *happily ever after* in the way God intended the marriage covenant to be.

Introduction

Wealth . . . a word that contains a sort of mysticism and magic . . . wealth is something that we desire, but is not necessarily easy to obtain. Of the billions of people on the planet, only a very few have proved successful at obtaining wealth. Why is this so? And more importantly, what must we do to become wealthy? The topic of wealth is an important one for so many people. Thousands (and still counting) of books and articles have been written about this subject. Does anybody really need another one?

Some years ago, in 2008, I reached what I consider to be the lowest point in my life. I had seen a succession of major accomplishments, and great failures. It felt like a roller coaster ride where I was taken to great heights, only to be thrown down shortly after. I didn't understand much of what was going on, and like many other people, I enjoyed taking credit for my past successes while blaming others for my failures. The feeling of emptiness and lack of purpose was so overwhelming that I couldn't see the path ahead. I could only wonder if my life would ever be different and, if so, what I should do differently to have a better future. That moment was a turning point for me, although the process of finally understanding who I am and what I should do took a bit more time.

This book is the outcome of a long analytical process, and the reason it is now published is that I believe that others will benefit by reading the conclusions and concepts I have outlined here. I was privileged to spend my life in several completely different economic systems. I was born, grew up, and started my professional career in Communist Romania, where I fully understood the fallacies of a corrupt system that had no respect for private initiative and individual freedom. But I also experienced the "wild capitalistic" years of transition from Communism to a free market economy—a period that brought confusion and frustration for some people, but also unexpected opportunities for others, including myself. I spent half of my adult life in Norway (misidentified by many as a "half-socialist" system), where private initiative coexists successfully with a strong, but still limited, government. And now I live in the United States, which has been for centuries (and will hopefully remain) the dream country for anybody who places a high value on individual freedom and a small government.

Why do I talk about wealth? As long as the distribution of wealth and the ever-increasing gap between the wealthy and nearly everyone else is a concern, there will always be opinions and theories as to why this happens. Perhaps our human nature is so complex that there is no final answer. I will nevertheless try to find one. My first important observation is that society is organized more around *behavioral patterns* than *individuals*. In other words, people seem to forfeit their uniqueness while struggling to fit into a mold that everybody else defines as acceptable. I will expand this idea later on.

While I will answer some questions about wealth and about how to become wealthy, I need first to clarify what this book is NOT about. It is not a book of financial advice. I have some basic education in macroeconomics and business administration, but I prefer to just call myself a "common-sensist." The book is not about how to invest money, and definitely not about how to get the highest return on financial investments. In fact, I will use very few numbers to illustrate its concepts. Also, although some sections of this book are dedicated to analyzing money and how money is used in the process of wealth creation, this is not a book about making more money. While most people are looking for a magic formula, the fact is that those who have become wealthy in a sustainable manner never applied a magic formula that made them wealthy overnight.

Here is what the book IS about. It explains how to build wealth through the diligent use of four *non*-financial resources to which every person on this planet has access. These resources are *creativity, time, knowledge*, and *opportunities*. This access is granted to everybody, regardless of their country, nationality, race, social status, or whatever else might be thought of as a "personal disadvantage." I hope to clearly explain the following important concepts:

- *money* is a reward for giving people what they need and want;

- *money* and *currency* are substantially different;

- *currency* (which is the right term for what we usually call *money*) is just an image without substance, necessary only to exchange for accumulating possessions that make a person truly wealthy;

- every person in this world has a *given right* to gain wealth, possess goods, and have dominion over a share of the world's resources;

- this right is given by each individual's fair access to four basic resources: creativity, time, knowledge, and opportunities;

- wealth is a consequence of consistent and wise use of these four resources over a long period of time, even over several generations.

While most people continue to look for the magic formula that will geometrically grow their stash of cash, I will prove that the true magic formula lies in the realm of personal choices and responsibility. Without a doubt, these are what make the entire difference between a *wealth maker* and a *wishful thinker*.

PART I

Wealth, Money,

and

Personal Finances

Chapter 1
Wealth and Money

If you were to conduct a survey to determine the priorities of life as defined by different people, you would surely discover that gaining wealth would rank pretty high. Whatever motivation lies behind the struggle to gain material possessions, we would all agree that a life in wealth is way better than a life in poverty. But when discussing wealth, this is probably the only thing that people would agree upon. Wealth is a very complex concept, and disagreements will crop up any time we try to answer questions like the following:

- What should be the role of material possessions in my life?

- What is the true level of "having enough"?

- Where is the borderline between "legitimate desire to have" and "greed"?

- Why is wealth so unevenly distributed on the Earth?

. . . and so on . . .

This book will join the fray with its own unique slant on the topic:

- being wealthy is a matter of responsibility and mindset;

- it is NOT a privilege given to a few;

- being wealthy is, rather, a right given to everybody.

What Is Wealth?

The Merriam-Webster Dictionary defines wealth as "abundance of valuable material possessions or resources." *Wikipedia* and many other resources would concur.

A useful definition, to be sure, but it needs a bit more elaboration.

1. A valuable possession can be easily exchanged. That is, the possessor has something that other people desire, need, or accept.

2. A valuable possession generates income to the possessor.

So here's my version: *Wealth* is the abundance of resources and possessions that are *easily exchangeable* and *generate income for the possessor.* All further discussion of wealth in this book will use this revised definition.

This concept strongly contradicts the definition commonly used these days—that wealth is a matter of *net worth*. According to the net worth theory, also known as the "wealth effect," you are wealthy when your belongings (improperly called "assets," like the house you live in, cars, stocks, shares in mutual funds) have a high value, so therefore, you can load yourself up with consumer debt because, after all, your "assets" are *more* valuable. This theory proved to be unsustainable during the last financial crisis, when most people believed they were wealthy just because the nominal prices of their homes kept rising. The borrowing carousel allowed them to refinance periodically at steadily increasing values. They were simply not aware that refinancing their own house at a higher value is nothing else but selling their own house to themselves at a higher price. While they were able to take out the gains as "equity" and enjoyed spending the money on consumables, they overlooked the fact that they had committed to pay the difference later on, with interest. Eventually, they drowned deeper and deeper in consumer debt. How did it go after a few years of people using their homes as ATMs? We all know the results.

This whole concept of the wealth effect seemed logical to me too, and I wholeheartedly supported it myself, for a time: "I can load up piles of debt just because I have the ability to make money by surfing a wave of 'paper wealth' creation." I had to learn the hard way that this is nothing more than an illusion.

When defining wealth, there are some other pragmatic ways to view it. For instance, Robert Kiyosaki, the author of the best-selling *Rich Dad, Poor Dad* series, defines wealth in relation to passive income over time. According to him, "Wealth is the period of time you can live maintaining your current living standard when you stop working." In other words, how many months can you live if you stop working and have no income from current work? People living from paycheck to paycheck have *zero wealth*. If they stop working, their income stops and they will not be able to maintain the same standard of living. On the other hand, there are people who possess *assets* (rental properties, dividend-paying stocks, etc.) that produce enough *income* to cover all their *expenses*. These are the people whom Kiyosaki calls *perpetually wealthy* because, even if they stop working, they will be able to maintain their standard of living in perpetuity. This approach may be somewhat different from what we all have learned—that a wealthy person is somebody who has lots of money. Therefore, the natural and obvious question to ask would be: Where is money in this definition?

The Misconception of Using Money in Defining Wealth

The fact remains that, despite perceived commonalities, money and wealth are not equivalent concepts, and they cannot be substituted for each other. *Wealth may include monetary possessions, but large monetary possessions are not necessary to be wealthy, and having money does not necessarily make you a wealthy person.*

Still, most of us make a direct connection between wealth and money, where money is understood as a sort of good or medium used for exchange. And indeed, though money is used for exchange of goods and services, equating wealth to money may be limiting and misleading, for several reasons. If we mistake money for the goods and services it can purchase, we fall into a major trap, and unfortunately, most of us do. I will provide many examples that illustrate that significant amounts of money do not necessarily guarantee wealth.

First: the equation of wealth and money creates the perception that a person with lots of money is a wealthy person, which is not always true. In one of his interviews, James Rickards, the best-selling author of *The Currency Wars* and *The Death of Money*, said, "Money is transitory, while wealth is permanent."

- A person with lots of money is wealthy only to the extent of the acceptance by others of that money. The moment other people start losing their confidence in that money, the wealth is significantly reduced. When the confidence in money totally disappears, there is no wealth.

- It is also a matter of supply and demand. Wealth expressed in monetary terms is preserved as long as there is a balance in the economy between the supply of money and the value of goods and services. When the supply of money exceeds the value of goods and services, the phenomenon is called *inflation*, and the pressure of the expanding money supply will push prices up. Throughout history, many countries experienced, during times of transition, hyperinflation. The Weimar Republic, the German republic established in 1919 as a result of the defeat of Germany in WWI, is the best-known example. A loaf of bread was sold for 1 mark in 1919, but just four years later, in 1923, the price of that same loaf was 100 billion marks. Money became so worthless that nobody really wanted it. The story is told of an older lady who was robbed in Berlin while she was carrying a lot of cash in a wheelbarrow. Nothing strange, you say; after all, it is like she was inviting a robbery. The funny thing is that the robber, after brutalizing her, dumped the money in the middle of the street and . . . ran away with the wheelbarrow! Regardless of whether the story is true or not, it illustrates what happens with highly inflated paper money: people have no interest in the money itself, only in tangible goods. Most countries in Central and Eastern Europe experienced high inflation during their transition from Communist to market economies. Many people found that their savings of a lifetime, considered to be a well-deserved cushion for retirement, were reduced in a few years to the value of a bag of groceries.

- Another circumstance where lots of money does not necessarily equate to being wealthy is the possession of significant amounts of so-called nonconvertible currency. A person residing in a country with a currency that is not widely accepted in the international markets may need to "convert" his monetary possessions. During this process, he may experience significant reduction of the value of his financial assets. The amount of goods he could buy in a destination country may be significantly lower than the amount of goods he could buy in his home country, although an official exchange rate would state otherwise. Currently (at the time of this writing), Argentina is enforcing a tight control on its own citizens' access to US dollars. While the official rate is between 7 and 8 pesos to 1 dollar, people who want to buy dollars need to pay, on the illegal black market, between 10 and 11 pesos per dollar. This means that the same number of pesos, while officially being equivalent to a certain number of US dollars, represents in fact 50 to 85 percent less when someone needs to get hold of US dollars. Or consider the reunification of Germany in the early 1990s. During this process, the former Communist East Germany (DDR) was a part of Germany. In order to restrict transfer of fortunes gained illegally by the Communist party leaders, certain restrictions for cash conversion were enforced. Communist Germany citizens were allowed to convert their old cash into DM (deutsche marks, the legal currency of West Germany in that time) at a rate of 1:1 only up to a limit of 4,000 DM. Further, bank savings and house loans were converted at a 2:1 ratio, while any other amount of cash, presumably speculative money, could be converted at a 3:1 ratio. Regardless of how wealthy a party leader was in Communist Germany, meaning regardless of how much DDR money he possessed, he could not freely transfer that wealth as a citizen of the new reunited Germany.

Second: the equation creates the feeling that all our problems will disappear if we would only make *more* money. This is completely wrong thinking, because most of our problems do not stem from *lack* of money, but rather from *lack of wisdom to properly use money*. The question is not *how much do you have*, but *what you do with what you have*. If you make the right choices and are a good manager of your assets and possessions, you will see your possessions increase. Likewise, if you make wrong choices and are a poor asset manager, you will be like a man with holes in his pockets . . . continually filling them but ending up with nothing.

If you are used to spending all the money you make, you will spend all the money you make, regardless of whether it's a lot or little. More money in the wallet simply means *more money to spend*. Without a change in mentality and proper financial counsel, if you are making $50,000 a year and spending $55,000 (where the 10 percent difference of $5,000 is covered by a credit card), you will spend $110,000 when your income increases to $100,000. As the revenues increase even more, you will have the feeling of achieving more, but instead you will just be sinking deeper and deeper into debt. In their book *Why We Want You to Be Rich*, Donald Trump and Robert Kiyosaki argue,

> The one problem money cannot solve is poverty. [. . .] The problem with throwing money at the issue of poverty is that

money only creates more poor people and keeps people poorer longer. The one true solution to worldwide poverty is financial education, not money.

Third: the equation makes us believe that a sudden increase in our finances will make us wealthy for the rest of our life. This is also as wrong as it can be. Statistics show that as many as 70 percent of lottery or cash prize winners find themselves in financial distress in just a few years. This is because they believe that the fortune wheel will always spin in their favor and therefore never change their "spend, spend, God will send" mentality.

This belief can also be observed in the case of professional athletes or artists—specially gifted people who make millions while using their gifts. Unfortunately, they believe that they will continue being in the spotlight for the rest of their life and will be able to cash in the same amounts of money year after year. Many celebrities end up in drama because they believe a big lie—that fans love *them*. The hard fact is that fans love their *gift*, not them. In the case of a popular musician, when trends shift and their music is not popular any more, people will look for the next star and abandon the old one. The same happens to athletic team fan favorites. When performance in the playing field decreases, he or she is replaced with somebody performing better. Many celebrities' lives turn into tragedies because they do not understand why the love of fans is not there anymore. In conclusion, large amounts of money gained in the short term are a blessing only as long as a significant part of the money is preserved and allocated to wise investments that generate reasonable income year after year, especially after the public "love" disappears. That would be the ideal time for a famous person to focus on using the gift in a meaningful way, rather than feeling sorrowful about the lost audience and finding refuge in depression, alcohol, or drugs. For instance, an athlete can be involved in coaching, or an artist can develop a teaching career.

Fourth: and maybe the most important of all—the equation creates a false connection between money and *significance*. Although we may be tempted to believe that people with money automatically feel significant, this is not true. Significance comes out of fulfillment and purpose, and there are plenty of people who feel miserable despite the fact that they have made lots of money and are still making more.

When you define your significance by setting a certain financial target, you may reach the target, but still feel insignificant. You may say, "I will feel important when I make my first million," but if there is no meaning or purpose as to *why* you want to make that million, you will just raise the stakes to a higher amount once you have reached it. One of the reasons for this is that you are defining achievement in a game where you are already at a disadvantage right from the start. While you are working hard to increase your income with some thousands or tens of thousands every year (US dollars, Euros, Canadian dollars, Swiss francs, or whatever other currency you operate with), a handful of people controlling that currency (to be more specific, the board of a central bank) has the power to create billions with a stroke of a pen—by simply adopting administrative measures and punching some numbers into a computer. Seen from *your* perspective, it is like working hard to get something, but when you get there, you didn't really get there— somewhat like a horse chasing a dangling carrot. Tony Robbins, the successful life coach and author, says in his seminars: "You should never define the game in a manner that is impossible to win."

Unfortunately, that is exactly what happens when you define your significance as relative to a level of net worth—you will never feel significant. In all the cases above, the false feeling of wealth given by money is created by having access to luxury goods and services and an increased credit limit. While we will delve more into the true nature of money in Chapter 4, it is important to always understand that wealth is strictly limited to those elements stated in the definition—an abundance of resources or material possessions that are valuable. And, as I have stated in our definition, when something is valuable, two things are meant: (1) it can be easily exchanged, because it is easily accepted by others, and (2) when it is possessed by somebody, it is generating income for the possessor.

Real Wealth vs. Paper Wealth

Before elaborating on the true nature of money (or *currency*, the usage we see nowadays) a bit further in this book, we have to agree that, if we define wealth in relation to exchangeable and income-producing possessions, we have to differentiate between assets that have *true intrinsic value* and assets that have value just because, at certain given times, there is a form of *general confidence* behind them.

The main difference is that real possessions, i.e., assets with intrinsic value, will always have an exchangeable value, regardless of times and seasons. On the other hand, paper assets that are backed only by general confidence have extremely volatile value because, when that confidence diminishes, much (if not all) of that value disappears. The best example is bonds issued by a corporation or a government. These bonds have a nominal value, but their price in the financial markets is determined by the market's confidence in that corporation's or government's ability to pay at the due date. This means that a bondholder's paper wealth can fluctuate very much, depending on the level of confidence.

The paradox is that, in times of financial boom, when paper assets are priced high in monetary terms, it seems that real assets have no value and people holding to tangibles are ridiculed. But when the financial markets bust, the real *hard assets* are the only ones that have a value. They may be harder to sell if one needs cash, but the value will always be there.

Understanding the "Luck" Factor

Another misconception that needs addressing is that *luck* plays an important role in distribution of wealth in the world. We talk in an envious manner about someone born "under a lucky star" or "with a silver spoon in his mouth," and we have a tendency to believe that some people are more fortunate than others. In a later chapter, I will analyze *opportunity* as a very important resource that is made available to each of us, and I will also look at the concept of *risk*— an element that is always associated with opportunities.

Wealthy people understand the importance of taking advantage of opportunities when they show up; additionally, they have developed the wisdom to manage the risks associated with each opportunity. They are risk takers to the degree that risks are kept at a reasonable level. This means that wealthy people experience failure from time to time, but they use failure as a learning experience to avoid future mistakes.

Tina Seelig, the executive director of Stanford Technology Ventures Program and a recognized teacher on entrepreneurship and innovation, dedicates a whole chapter of her book *What I Wish I Knew When I Was 20* to clarifying the connection between hard work and luck. She wrote, "We often hear inspiring stories about people who start with nothing and by virtue of incredibly hard work are able to draw luck their way" (p. 118). The fact is that you need to put yourself in a position to make yourself lucky or to attract luck. Looking at others, you may say, "Wow, that person was so lucky," but if you really look at their story, that person most likely has done a number of things to position himself or herself and/or attract luck.

If you want to position yourself for wealth, you'll need to meet a lot of people, you'll have to read a lot of educational and insightful materials, you'll need to listen to and learn from people who have "been there, done that," and you'll need to be observant and take mental notes on your surroundings and all that is happening. It is remarkable the number of things that happen when you dare to get out of your comfortable surroundings!

Furthermore, there is a special connection between attitude and luck. In the same chapter, Tina Seelig says, "Lucky people also tend to be optimistic and to expect good things to happen to them. This becomes a self-fulfilling prophecy because even when things don't go as expected, lucky people find ways to extract positive outcomes from the worst situations" (p. 122).

This is also confirmed by *Scientific American* in an article called "As Luck Would Have It":

> Lucky people smile twice as often and engage in more eye contact than unlucky people do, which leads to more social encounters which generates more opportunities. [. . .] They're more likely to notice chance opportunities even when they're not expecting them. [. . .] Finally, but even in the face of adversity, lucky people turn bad breaks into good fortune. (*www.scientificamerican.com / article / as-luck-would-have-it*)

Accepting the idea that hazard plays a role in your life will cause you to focus on the wrong elements. Believing the lie that you are less fortunate than others will lead you down a dangerous, fatalistic path. Your thoughts of failure will transform into words, and you will start making statements like "nothing works for me," "I was born to lose," "I am a failure," "I will never perform like others," and so on. Further, your actions become limited, and you will become stuck and afraid of taking advantage of opportunities because you think, "it will go south anyway." You will end up victimizing yourself and blaming others for your failures, instead of using them as opportunities to learn.

Finally, there is also a connection between hard work and luck. As Robert Herjavec, the successful entrepreneur and *Shark Tank* investor, said in his interview with Fanny Kiefer, "The reality is that the harder you work, the luckier you get". (*www.youtube.com/watch?v=__uwQXeDNt8*)

The "Excuse" and the "Inequality in Opportunity" Factors

Another reason why it easy to reject the idea that wealth is available for anybody is our focus on what we do *not* have. Looking at others' advantages and easier start and comparing our own situation with theirs, we conclude that we do not have the same advantages; therefore, we end up believing that we cannot achieve what others achieve because they have what it takes, and we don't.

"Inequality in opportunity" seems to be one of most debated topics in mainstream media today, and there are many opinions stating that young people born in rich families are better positioned for success. And, of course, all kinds of statistics are used in support of the argument that people are given different opportunities in life. What really surprises me is not the conclusion; after all, observing that people born in rich families have a better start than those born in poor families is simply a common-sense observation that shouldn't require any study. But I *am* surprised by two things.

One is the fact that statistics are used to change the focus from "inequality in opportunity" (which is about the starting point) to "inequality in outcome" (which is about the end result). The statement that many people born in rich families succeed while few people born in poor families can show the same achievements is a factual statement about the end result. Linking the end result (success) directly to the starting point (opportunity) is very manipulative because it ignores the fact that people are individuals who develop behavioral patterns and make choices along the way.

The second element that surprises me is that these statistics are used to support the need to provide "equality in outcome." Simply put: because some people succeed more than others, something must be done to make sure that more people born in poor families succeed. What needs to be understood here is that people born into rich families have an inheritance because somebody in their family tree, be it parents, grandparents, or even older ancestors, made a deliberate choice to break out of poverty. No matter how wealthy a person is now, there was a time in history, maybe one generation back, maybe several generations, when someone took the first step of building wealth—from nothing.

While people born in poor families will have a harder time, an undeniable fact, the true equality in opportunity is the chance given to anyone to break out of the family tree of poverty. According to Tom Corley, the best-selling author of *Rich Habits*, no fewer than 85 percent of American millionaires are self-made, first-generation rich. Instead of focusing on others having an easier start, you should rather ask yourself: "What can I do to make sure that I break the cycle and leave to my children and grandchildren a legacy that positions them better than my parents positioned me?"

I have mentioned before, and I will state this basic principle several times in this book: it is never a matter of *what you have* and *what you do not have*; it is always a matter of *what you do with what you have at any given time*. Comparing yourself with others will cause you to make excuses for why you cannot achieve great things in your life. Here are some of the most frequently used excuses:

- I was born in a poor country; wealth can be gained only in richer countries.

- I grew up in the wrong part of the city, in a neighborhood where only bad things happen.

- I grew up in a dysfunctional family.

- My parents never encouraged me or saved any money to pay for my education.

You can always find reasons why other people can generate and accumulate wealth while you cannot do anything else but stay stuck in an average, middle-class life. As Pastor Randy Morrison of Speak the Word Church International always says, "Excuses are the crutches of the uncommitted." All it takes is some extra effort, understanding, and a willingness to accept that you are the one responsible for your own future.

Wealth and Your Social Environment

Wealthy people do not surround themselves with ignorant people. This may sound like an arrogant statement, but when using the descriptor "ignorant," I do not mean "stupid." Later in this book I will dedicate an entire section to the concept of *ignorance*. I personally believe that each person is gifted with the ability to think, at least at the common-sense level. As I will explain later on, ignorance refers to a personal choice to avoid or dodge away from knowledge.

Wealthy people are selective when it comes to persons they dedicate their time to. Although the vanity factor is very much involved when aspiring to certain social circles, wealthy people seek to be in the presence of like-minded people, where there's something to be learned. Wealthy people talk frequently about ideas and opportunities and how to transform these into wealth.

We are always a result of our environment. Like plants, which need the right soil, humidity, and temperature to grow, we humans need the right environment in order to thrive. Consuming our finite stores of time by spending them with people who choose to remain ignorant is simply a complete waste. Just to avoid any doubt, I do not support the concept that wisdom increases in accordance with the amount of money and rank one has in society, for there are thousands of examples that prove the contrary. At the same time, there are millions of wise people in what we define as the lower classes.

Some wealthy people are both humble and generous, involved in helping others. Still, they prefer to dedicate their time to exchanging ideas with people who share their thoughts and ideas, rather than surrounding themselves with people who have a poverty mentality. Their life is about turning *ideas* into *wealth*, not about being poor. As a result, when interacting with other people, they do not focus on personality or grouping people into "likeable" or "unlikeable" categories, but rather choose to respect others' abilities, strengths, and wisdom.

When you make a commitment to become wealthy, you should, on a regular basis, perhaps yearly, evaluate your contacts and eliminate those people in your life who are just consumers of your resources. Most likely, you will find certain people who do not contribute anything positive to your life, having their own issues and dramas and forcing their problems onto you. You will most likely end up feeling guilty for not involving yourself enough in sorting out *their* problems. This may sound like selfishness, but it's not. This is about responsibility and taking care of resources that are available to everyone—in this case, to yourself.

Breaking up with acquaintances is not always easy. You will face pressure from several sides. One is that there's a great chance for you to become a gossip topic. If some of these people try to reconnect with you, you will be met with resentful remarks like "Who do you think you are?" or "Did you forget where you started from?" And while you work on building new connections, you may very well feel lonely for a while. As there is always a difference between being *alone* and being *lonely*, this is an ideal time for introspection, an opportunity to discover your true self. In addition, it frees up the necessary time to search for and build the contact network that will take you to the next level.

Chapter 2
Four Resources for Wealth Making

Every human being, regardless of their place of birth, age, race, or social status, has access to four resources: *creativity, time, knowledge,* and *opportunities.*

- Creativity

Creativity is the power to innovate, imagine, and create new things. It is also the power to extend or expand existing ideas and concepts beyond current boundaries. As I will show later on, there is a difference between *making* and *creating.* While making is about bringing something out of other elements that already exist, creating is about bringing to reality something that never existed before. Leonardo da Vinci *made* a painting out of canvas and paint, but he *created* Mona Lisa. Ferrari is a company *making* cars out of existing materials (steel, aluminum, rubber, plastic, fabric), but using the design *created* by Sergio Pininfarina. Creativity and ideas reside in every one of us in the form of talents and gifts.

- Time

Time is the currency of the world. Everything that surrounds us is a result of someone's efforts and time. Time is available to all of us and is the only resource that is evenly distributed. Not one of us can buy more time, make more time, or increase or decrease it. Twenty-four hours a day are given to each of us—the richest and the poorest, the strongest and the weakest, and the youngest and the oldest. What we choose to do with the available time makes the entire difference.

- Knowledge

Although the area of *knowledge* seems to be very complex, it is important to note that knowledge has become much more available during the last decades, both in terms of access and cost. This area is defined by three levels—information, knowledge, and wisdom. While information represents facts about something or somebody, knowledge is about applying information. Further, wisdom, as the ultimate level of knowledge, is insight and experience added to knowledge.

While you can argue that costs of formal education have constantly increased, there are many examples of people who, not having the means to pay for tuition and other costs associated with education, gained knowledge by becoming self-learners. Indeed, certain professions cannot be practiced without a formal education and degree, but much knowledge is available on the Internet, in books and other forms of published materials, as well as through specialized seminars and conferences.

- Opportunities

Every single day, we witness or discover problems that need solving. Every solution is an *opportunity* waiting to be noticed. But we overlook these opportunities, settling on the position that things have always been and will always be the way they are. We do not take a moment to think about why we do the things we do and what can be done differently. Opportunities are everywhere, but they have to be discovered.

* * *

Anybody can see that these four resources are generally available. Every single person on this Earth has access to them. Exercise and application of these resources may be easy for some and more difficult for others, but no one is denied access to them. This is precisely why I will demonstrate in the following chapters that building wealth is not a matter of having or not having money, but is rather a matter of using all four resources in the right way by means of the following:

- eliminating *waste*;

- *spending* with a clear purpose;

- focusing on *investing*.

As long as we have defined *wealth* as "abundance of valuable possessions" and choose to see *valuable* as "exchangeable" and "producing income," we can conclude that wealth is ultimately generated by a constant flow of income, where money is used as an exchange platform for the other resources used to acquire income-producing possessions. This will be more clearly illustrated in the next chapter.

Chapter 3
Waste, Spend, or Invest?

The concept of a resource was discussed in detail in the previous chapter. In order to understand the aspects of how we use resources, I have to clarify some basic ideas.

Resources and Their Usage

On a daily basis, we are in contact with different types of resources, and normally we associate the concept of a *resource* with "something that can be transformed into something valuable." When we identify resources in our lives, we immediately recognize tangible resources, like commodities, utilities, and goods. The main characteristic of these tangible resources is that, when in our possession, they can make our life better and more comfortable. Therefore we perceive them as primary resources. And this is also the reason we are tempted to see money as a tangible resource, because money has the same basic function—it allows us to *buy things*.

After giving it more thought, we can define or identify nontangible resources as well, such as information, skills, relationships, and time. We perceive these as secondary resources because, when possessing them, we are able to exchange them for primary resources. For example, if we possess information and have developed skills in certain areas (industries), we can use them in our professional life. When we make such skills and information available for an employer, we get money that can be used to buy goods and services, which in turn make our life better. When resources are in our possession, we can use them in one of the following three ways:

- waste;

- spend;

- invest.

As you can see, I did not include *consume* on this list. Later, when I analyze these three ways of using resources, you will see that "consuming resources" is a general idea that covers all three specific usages. When consumed, any resource can be wasted, spent, or invested.

Wasting Resources

Most often we associate waste with inefficiency, refuse, lost value, or something undesirable. In relation to resources, we understand *wasting* as "release of a resource without having any benefit from its usage."

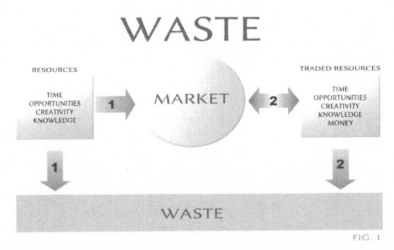

WASTE

RESOURCES   TRADED RESOURCES

TIME OPPORTUNITIES CREATIVITY KNOWLEDGE   **1**   MARKET   **2**   TIME OPPORTUNITIES CREATIVITY KNOWLEDGE MONEY

1   **2**

WASTE

FIG. 1

As illustrated in this drawing, all resources can be wasted. We can waste them directly, when they are already in our possession, or we can waste resources that we have purchased on the market. For instance, if you are a regular employee, you can waste your own time in front of your TV—this is a resource that you waste directly. But if you are a business owner and your employees have to wait for some hours for some supplies that you forgot to order, you are wasting *their* time—a resource that your business (and ultimately, you) pay for. We can identify dozens of situations where we spend or sow resources and fail to reap a harvest. Here are just a few examples:

- *Disorganization*: When we are disorganized and do not keep track of our current "stuff," we end up buying a second identical item, simply because we have no recollection of where we stored the original item.

- *Poor record keeping*: When we do not keep our files and documents in order, we find ourselves redoing much of the work previously done.

- *Buying more than we need*: When we buy perishable groceries in quantities larger than we are able to consume, inevitably we are forced to throw away a large part of them.

- *Idleness*: Waste occurs when we sit in front of the TV for several hours, jumping from one channel to another without a purpose or means to an end.

- *Energy inefficiency*: Waste occurs when we continue to power equipment long after we have finished using it.

- *Laziness*: We are wasteful when, for example, we drive around for an extra half hour trying to get somewhere because we failed to use the GPS or refused to ask for directions.

Obviously, a direct connection exists between waste and efficient usage of resources. More waste leads to achieving less with the same resources, significantly decreasing efficiency. This is why eliminating or at least reducing wasteful use of resources should be our first priority.

Climbing the social ladder by making more money or developing a business (increasing the volume and operating at a higher level or larger scale) will have only limited benefits if resources are not used in an efficient manner. This applies to both your personal life and professional life. If you are a business owner, you may think that simply expanding the business will, in itself, take care of all problems. But without a clear focus, as the business develops and revenues increase, you will eventually discover that you are just producing more waste. The process of change and adjustment in your life should start with a careful analysis of how you use available resources, followed by a strong commitment to eliminating waste.

Spending Resources

Although we normally associate the action of spending with money, this category of use of resources can be analyzed in a much wider perspective. Spending accounts for most of the circumstances in which we use resources. When we are in possession of certain resources, we release them with the purpose of getting something in return. This is why we can see *spending* as "release of a resource to get something in exchange or having an immediate benefit from its usage."

As illustrated below, we use resources for exchange, and we even use money as a medium of exchange. The money we get into our hands is used to buy consumable goods. These may last a few years, and because they make our life better, we consider them to be assets. But still, they finally depreciate and need to be replaced.

SPEND

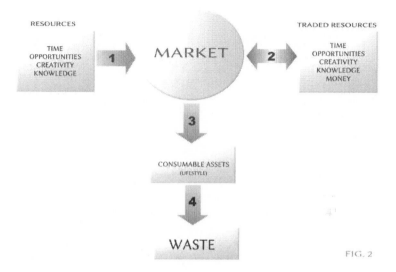

FIG. 2

Seen in a wider perspective, when we spend our resources, we get in exchange goods and services that meet our physical, material, emotional, and intellectual needs. Here are some examples:

- A family spends money to buy a house, pay a mortgage, or pay rent to meet the basic need for shelter.

- A man spends money to buy a car, which meets his material need for safe and convenient transportation and, in some cases, his emotional need to display power and success.

- We spend money on books, movies, and music to fulfill a desire to be enlightened, educated, or entertained, which most often satisfies our intellectual and emotional needs.

- Parents spend time with their kids to meet their own and their children's emotional and social needs.

- Ladies meet at an exclusive café and spend money not only to get a cup of coffee, but also to fulfill a social need: to see and be seen (let alone to catch up on gossip).

- Families and friends spend money dining out not only to satisfy their basic need for food but also to develop mutual relationships and to be entertained.

- Employees spend time at their workplaces in exchange for a paycheck they can use later on.

The concept of spending is somewhat intuitive: a resource is released and something is received immediately in exchange for the resource that was released. The benefit is immediate. At first look, differences in the definitions of spending and wasting seem to be obvious. Wasting is about releasing resources while getting *nothing* in return, while spending is about releasing resources while getting *something* in return. The details, however, reveal that the line between wasting and spending is pretty thin, and even more, there is a gray area that encompasses both wasting and spending. This is mainly because while we may get something (qualifying that exchange as spending), it is hard to agree upon the value of what is received in exchange. As described in Chapter 1, value is always a matter of perception, and defining a use of resources as waste or spending depends on that perceived value. Let us look at some examples.

- Impulse shopping

A situation that most of us can relate to is being sold something that we did not really need. We just happened to be in that place at that time while we stood in front of that very persistent salesman, and his offer seemed to be a very good deal. Did we get something? Yes, we did indeed get something, but the strong regretful feeling we experienced the day after is proof that we wasted rather than spent.

- Emotional shopping

Emotional shopping is a reaction usually triggered by a stressful event or situation, or the disappointing behavior of someone very close to us. It can even be triggered by boredom or a lack of purpose. A typical situation is when, following a dispute or the misconduct of her spouse, a lady runs out to the mall. After a two-hour raid using all the available funds on the credit cards, she returns home overloaded with stuff and suffused with a sweet feeling of revenge. But also with a few bags of new garments that were not needed in the first place.

- Buying things that feed our own ego

There is a saying that "the difference between boys and men lies in the size and price of the toys they are buying." A car is a typical example. While women are mainly concerned about a car's functionality, reliability, and safety, men will have an additional dimension of concern: the car has to represent *them*. Therefore, they will buy and proudly drive a brand new $60,000 car. That is not about the basic need for transportation; after all, we can get a pretty decent car with four wheels and a steering wheel that can take us from A to B and keep us safe and dry for a few thousand dollars. Nor is it about comfort, because nowadays a $25,000 car will provide a pretty high level of comfort. The difference between $25,000 and $60,000 is nothing more than the price to be paid for "showing off" or keeping up with the Joneses.

- Working for low compensation

Sometimes we accept work or provide services for a lower compensation than the actual value of our own efforts invested in a venture. In most cases, there is a legitimate reason for such acceptance: an expectation of additional ulterior benefits, often even backed by a promise given by the person receiving the work or services in the first place. A typical example is when a new joint venture is started and one of the partners is promised a compensation for his work in the form of stocks. Success of the venture will make him consider his efforts as "well spent," maybe even "a good investment," as I will describe in the next section. Failure of the venture will make all those efforts wasted.

Investing Resources

Mentioning the word *investment* leads immediately to the idea of finances. To invest money means that you put some money into a business venture (or real estate, bank deposits, bonds, commodities, securities, mutual funds), and after a while you get your money back with a certain return. Again, I would bring in the same wider perspective, not limiting the investment concept to just money and finances.

I mentioned that spending gives immediate benefits when releasing resources, whatever those resources may be: financial, time, information. In a similar way, investing is also about using resources and getting benefits; the difference is that, in this case, the benefits are not immediate, but returned in the future, and their value is higher than the initial resource released. Therefore, I define *investing* as "release of a resource to get a future flow of benefits whose total value is higher than the resources released."

The figure illustrates this concept very well. When resources are in our hands (including money) (steps 1 and 2), we invest them (step 3), meaning that we buy income-producing assets. These assets generate revenues (step 4) that can be used for new trades and new investments (step 5) or to buy consumable assets that make our life better (step 6). As the income-producing assets continue to accumulate, we build wealth (step 7).

INVEST

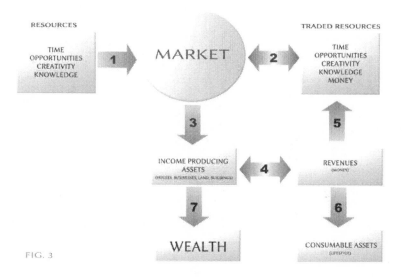

FIG. 3

When talking about finances, it's easy to understand the concept of putting a bit of money into an investment vehicle and getting a return on that investment. Here are a few examples:

- making a bank deposit will return interest;

- purchasing a property and renting it out can generate a cash flow that represents the return on investment;

- creating and maintaining a portfolio of stocks listed on the stock exchange can generate dividends (in addition to potential stock price appreciation);

- bonds (debt securities) and money market certificates provide return of the money with interest;

- buying commodities (metals, copper, iron core, oil, coffee, sugar, salt, rice) when prices are expected to increase gives opportunities to make profits when the commodities are sold at a later date (of course, the reverse is also true: if the prices decrease, there is a loss);

- derivative markets for stocks and commodities (e.g. options, futures) create gain opportunities for experienced investors with higher appetite for risk.

Each of the above methods of investing has associated levels of risks and rewards. As a rule, the higher the risk, the higher potential for reward. The purpose of this book is not to describe or analyze financial investments; there are thousands of available resources for these topics—books, magazines, newspapers, TV programs, specialized web pages with newsletters. These are available to everyone and should be carefully researched to determine which methods of investment are most suitable for your own financial growth. Two important aspects to have in mind about investing resources are the following:

- once released, the invested resource will generate a future flow of returned benefits;

- the accumulated value of the future benefits will exceed the initial value of the resource released.

As you can see, there is a difference between *capital gain* (which is buying an asset for the purpose of selling later at a higher price) and *return on investment* (which is a constant future flow of benefits). This is why, when I look at investing resources and their benefits, I will consider any form of benefits, not limiting benefits to financial returns. Time can be invested in acquiring knowledge or developing skills, and that knowledge or those skills can later be used multiple times. Sometimes you can trade them directly for money to an employer; other times you can use them for networking or for developing a certain type of relationship. When you gain the knowledge, you may be able to discover new opportunities. Limiting your understanding of benefits to financial returns will definitely slow your process of gaining wealth.

Additionally, there are a couple of non-financial examples to consider:

- Education

If we consider education costs apart from tuition and the direct costs associated with living during study years, education is primarily a matter of investing *time*. Young people dedicate their time to educate themselves, having in mind future benefits in the forms of career opportunities, future salary, or, if they choose to be entrepreneurs, better management and leadership skills. This is not valid only for young people; it applies to older people as well. As they learn more during their professional life, they will reap the same types of benefits.

Having said that, we have to be aware of one aspect, one related to the costs of education. Many say that education, due to its importance, should be acquired at all costs, and the strength of a nation is measured by the educational level of its people. While this statement contains a lot of truth, we need to put it in the right context. We have to understand that the only education worth paying for is the education allowing us to acquire skills that the market is willing to pay for. This is the reason we have today millions of people with college degrees and an overwhelming amount of student debt who cannot find suitable positions in the job market. Many young people were trapped into the belief that a college degree is all that it takes to access a well-paid job, and consequently, they went to college and graduated. They are now stuck with tens of thousands of dollars in student loans with few job prospects, if any at all.

This mismatch between available skills and market demand is the root cause of this paradox: millions of educated people have problems finding jobs, and yet so many companies complain of not being able to fill their positions because applicants lack necessary skills. US authorities run a program called H1B that opens annually for over 100,000 working visas and allows American companies to hire foreign individuals because there are not enough people in the US with required skills.

So education is important, but if the market is not willing to pay for the knowledge you acquire and the skills you develop, then we are talking about mastering a *hobby*, and you should not pay for that education (let alone the even worse scenario of acquiring a student loan debt). As an example, it makes no sense to get a college degree in philosophy or history unless you want to dedicate your career to teaching in those areas or work in a field where that knowledge is paid for. Having a genuine interest in philosophy and history is good for you as a person because it opens your mind and makes it possible to see things from different perspectives. In different social contexts, you will have the chance to actively participate in any related conversation, and this will make you feel more confident.

But it makes sense to pay high tuition and other educational costs only if, after graduation, you will be able to collect revenue from using the knowledge you have gained. If you have no intention to profess in the field, the extent of your investment in that field should be books, DVDs, and any other study materials that will keep it just a hobby. Unfortunately, too many young people are forced to start their careers waiting tables or flipping burgers while carrying a heavy student loan burden on their shoulders for a master's degree that brings them . . . nowhere.

- Relationships

Interpersonal relationships require a bit of dedicated time, and in most cases, this is an investment rather than an expense (spending). The benefits of long-term relationships, impossible to express in monetary terms, are of such value that time dedicated to building relationships cannot be seen as anything but an investment. You can think, for instance, of the relationship between parents and their children. As all children need validation and encouragement from their parents, dedicating quality time to this type of relationship will definitely influence a child's self-worth, self-esteem, and self-confidence.

* * *

I hope you now have a clear understanding of these three ways of using resources. It should be clear that we do not *consume* the resources we possess—we do one of the three things: waste, spend, or invest.

In the following chapters, we will look more closely at the four resources I have described in the previous chapter (creativity, time, knowledge, and opportunities), and I will analyze what it means to waste, to spend, or to invest them. As mentioned in the Introduction, I will prove that wealth is a matter of using these available resources in the right manner. But before doing so, I will clarify in the next two chapters some aspects related to money and a wealth mindset.

Chapter 4
Money and Currency

What Is Money? What Is Currency?

I started thinking about the true nature of money some years ago during a layover at Heathrow Airport in London. After I bought a few souvenirs, the cashier gave me my change: a 5-pound note, together with some coins. Having this banknote in my hand, I knew I had a small amount of British "money" to spend—a bit over 5 pounds. It was not the first time I had been in possession of a British banknote, but this time I noticed something I hadn't noticed before. Taking a closer look at the note, I read a very intriguing statement: "I promise to pay the bearer on demand the sum of 5 pounds."

That was both confusing and intriguing. "Hold on a second," I said to myself. Continuing in that vein, I thought, "Something is strange here. I was convinced that the lady in the store gave me 5 pounds. But she didn't. She gave me a piece of paper (with a nice print of Her Majesty the Queen, indeed, but still a piece of paper) that says that I have to go to the Bank of England if I want to get my 5 pounds."

If I had gone back to the store and asked the cashier what she had given to me, she would have surely answered, "I gave you 5 pounds." I am positive that she was also convinced that she had given me 5 pounds, not just a piece of paper. As I used that banknote to purchase a magazine and some snacks before I boarded the next plane, the cashier in the newspaper kiosk was also most probably convinced that I had given him 5 pounds. But if the 5-pound bill in my hand was not 5 pounds, only a *promise*, where were the 5 pounds? Obviously, they were not in that paper. There must be some form of value in that piece of paper that made me accept it in the same way as I would have received 5 pounds. And I could not be wrong, because the whole of Great Britain and the rest of the world accept the same paper as 5 pounds.

Without being able to answer for myself, at that time, the question "What is money?", I could figure out one thing: we were not passing 5 pounds from one to another, as we all believed. We were passing just a piece of paper stating a promise: that by taking this paper to the Bank of England, one could get one's 5 pounds. So, the 5-pound value must be somewhere hidden behind the general and unquestionable acceptance of that piece of paper, not in the paper itself.

This conclusion contradicted strongly the definition of money I learned in school. Growing up in a Communist system (Romania of the 1970s and 1980s), we were taught two main things: "money was invented to replace barter" and "money is merchandise accepted by everybody in exchange for goods and services." These definitions made sense, and at that time I accepted them. Trying to imagine a barter-based society, it is obvious that money makes everybody's life easier. Instead of wasting a lot of time trying to find barter partners, everybody could use money as intermediate "goods."

But sitting there at Heathrow Airport, after compiling all this information, I found everything to be contradictory—money cannot be merchandise, because merchandise is "something of substance that has value in itself." We use money today in its physical form as banknotes and coins. Banknotes are printed on paper, and there is no relationship between value and the quantity of material substance used to produce the banknote. The banknotes are pretty similar in size (relatively small differences between denominations), but the *values* are very different. A $100 bill is just slightly bigger than a $1 bill. So, if the same merchandise (paper and ink) can produce either the value of one dollar or the value of one hundred dollars, paper money cannot be merchandise.

What about the money in our bank accounts and on our credit cards? With these, there is even less substance, not even paper and ink. A magnetic strip on a piece of plastic can contain anything numerical; the same applies to hard disks and memory chips of bank computer systems. If we go to the bank to withdraw our money, we will get the same pieces of paper that contain a *promise*.

I started to look at coins. The problems are exactly the same as for paper notes. If I take a coin to the store, I get something for it. It may not be much, but the person in the store will accept it. And, if I put more coins together, I can get more goods. But if that coin is destroyed to the point that the imprint is no longer recognizable, the seller will not accept it. It is still the same metal and has still the same weight. The difference is the imprint; the difference is the *image*. It is not the metal itself, but the quarter image that makes the quarter. Obviously, none of our existing money, be it paper notes, coins, or numbers in bank accounts, can be *merchandise!*

Thinking about these things, I was not surprised by the realization that some of the things I learned in the Communist school system were wrong. After all, economic theories are always subject to political interpretation, and as long as I considered Communist policies to be wrong, all their economics teaching might also be wrong. What surprised me was the fact that the more I tried to figure out what money is, the more confused I became. I continued searching, trying to find other definitions in different lexicons and dictionaries, such as *Wikipedia* and *The Merriam-Webster Dictionary*, where money is defined as "an object," "a medium of exchange," "a unit of account," or "a store of value."

A *medium* should be something that *flows*, or *carries something*. Money indeed moves, but what does it carry? Having money will allow you to go to places and do things. People with money can do either good or bad things, because money can be used for good or for evil. Money can flow in one direction or another, but there is no "good" or "evil" content in it—it is just a matter of what money is used for. I felt that there was something missing. It was still impossible for me to grasp the concept of money beyond that image we carry in our wallets and bank statements. I kept asking myself: "Where is the money?"

And this entire search continued until I learned the difference between *money* and *currency*. While *money* is indeed *goods with intrinsic value* that can be exchanged for other goods or services, for *currency* there is nothing more behind the image—currency is just the *image created in our minds*. This is how I finally understood that *currency, the form of money we use today, is a generally accepted reflection of perceived value*.

Another important dimension of a currency is that its true nature is *debt*. Yes, currencies of the world are *promises to pay*—and that is debt! They are first created by a central bank as a promise to pay; then they are lent out to banks. Banks use the currencies in two ways: buying bonds (issued by governments, states, and municipalities for covering public expenses) and using the fractional reserve mechanism to create new currency as loans to the private sector (corporations and individuals).

That is also why there is a constant need for debt increase in the society. Most currency is created as debt in the banking system, through the fractional reserve mechanism, and because those amounts have to be paid back with interest, it means that more currency has to be in the system later on—to cover both the principal (the amount created initially) and the applicable interest. Therefore, all the currency that represents interest needs also to be created as new debt, in addition to all earlier incurred debt. The consequence is that our entire financial system based on paper money (or promises to pay)—which is totally different from a system based on money with intrinsic value—*requires a constant increase of debt in order to exist*.

From now on in this book, I will continue using the term *money*, although it is not the right term. As I have explained above, the right term to be used is *currency*. The main difference between money and currency is that *money* represents a *store of value*, maintaining its *purchasing power*, while *currency* doesn't—it is not a store of value and does not maintain purchasing power. Every time I use the term *money*, I will basically mean *currency*. Still, I choose to say *money*, because this is the most used concept for coins, banknotes, and the numbers in our bank accounts.

The sooner you understand the difference between money and currency, the faster you will start building real wealth. This definition of money as a "generally accepted reflection of perceived value" contains several components. Let us look at them one by one.

- Money is an image.

Money is not a substance, merchandise, or medium. Money is just a reflection, regardless of the physical form that is shown on paper (banknotes), metal (coins), plastic (cards), or electronically in bank accounts. Money reflects something.

- Money reflects a *perceived value*.

Most of the things around us, tangible or intangible, are measured and evaluated in money as the most commonly understood scale of values. When we express something in monetary terms, we express our perceived value of that thing, be it tangible or intangible. If something is important to us, we perceive it as being highly valuable, and we express it as being "worth a lot of money." Something that has less importance will be perceived as having low value and "worth less money."

- The image is *generally accepted*.

Anybody can design and print his own money, but it will not be accepted as a payment method. The official legal tenders are the only generally accepted images of value. We can try to buy something by paying with Monopoly© bills, but we have no chance of those bills being accepted or of getting anything in return.

How Money Occurred

Money occurred in the earliest stages of society when people were facing the difficulties involved in barter trade of goods. To make that exchange easier, they developed a scale of values based on the ratio between *supply* and *demand*. When somebody needed something, that something was *valuable*. If many people had the same need, the aggregated need of different individuals generated demand. Further, when somebody perceived that demand, they worked to produce something for the market that satisfied the need. That generated supply.

Therefore, money is an important part of the market system, because that is the place where goods and services are exchanged. Still, it's important to understand that the first money was not created by any government, but originated as a creation of the market—meaning that many individuals considered it to be acceptable as a medium of exchange.

But the ancient kings and rulers of those days saw this as a wonderful opportunity to take control of this exchange and positioned themselves thus: "Because it is difficult for you to exchange goods and services in barter form, we will give you something that will make your life easier. We will make some pieces of metal that you value (gold, silver) and we will call it money. We are the only ones who have the right to issue money, and, in exchange for the convenience we provide to you, we will take a share of the exchanges you perform with each other—we will call it taxes." And they produced coins out of metal, something that had intrinsic value and that could be easily recognized and accepted.

You may argue that this is a very simplified theory of the occurrence of money, and indeed it is. But in its simplicity, this theory illustrates the foundation on which authorities issue money. Things have become much more complicated since the days when a king was minting gold and silver—we have now central banks, regulatory bodies, and all kinds of committees and institutions. But the principle is still the same: authorities of a country (for instance, government) appoint an institution (a central bank) to release into the market a form of legal tender that is covered (guaranteed) with only one single security—the authorities' ability to collect taxes.

Especially in modern times, the value of currency is no longer backed by gold or silver, only by the authorities' decree that the pieces of paper we have in our wallet or the funds reflected in our bank statement is the only legal form of payment. This kind of money is known as *fiat currency*, and the definition applies to practically all monies in the world.

How We Should Relate to Money

Understanding the true nature of currency (an image, a reflection of perceived value) will make it possible for you to understand wealth and relate to money in a more realistic manner. The first thing you need to be aware of is the fact that today's currencies cannot be directly converted into something tangible. Of course, tangible goods are valued in monetary terms and can be purchased with currencies, but this is only based on supply and demand of those goods, without any direct conversion between tangible goods and currency.

This means that if you have $1,000 in your wallet or bank account, you can do something with it only as long as you find somebody willing to accept that $1,000 as payment for the goods or services they sell. But if there is nobody willing to take that money because of lack of trust or whatever other reason, you are simply stuck with *nothing*. You can never go to the Federal Reserve with the $1,000 and ask for *something* of equivalent value in return, because there is nothing tangible in the Federal Reserve that equates to that value. Neither can you go to the European Central Bank with 1,000 euros and ask for something tangible of equivalent value in return, because there is nothing there either that equates to that value.

Today's money is called currency mainly because it has to *flow* in order to generate economic activity. Every person's acceptance of money as payment keeps currency flowing. When the acceptance stops, the whole flow stops. Confidence is the factor that keeps the flow going.

While I was involved in some projects in Russia in 1992 and 1993, I noticed that, at that time, most of the Russian economy was based on cash payments in US dollars. The nouveaux riches of that day did not have much confidence in rubles, the local currency, and many restaurants and retail units were operating exclusively in US dollars. One of my friends, very familiar with the local business environment, mentioned to me that unofficial reports revealed that no less than one-third of the paper dollars in circulation were counterfeit. Still, this didn't seem to bother anybody. At that time, Russian confidence in rubles was so low so that they were willing to take a 33 percent chance on getting fake dollar bills rather than genuine rubles.

But there is another fundamental difference between money and currency, and this is revealed when a transaction occurs. As long as money represents a *real asset*, any transaction based on money is an exchange based on *valuable assets*. The selling entity gives away goods or services and gets in return the buyer's money, which is a real asset. The buying entity has to give up a real asset in order to purchase the desired goods and services. The transaction is finalized because the seller has received an asset.

In the transaction illustrated below, Jim has an asset (the TV set) and John has another asset (money with intrinsic value). When they exchange, Jim gets the money and John gets the TV set. Both Jim and John started with assets and ended up with assets. The transaction was valuable for both of them because Jim valued the money more than the TV set he possessed, and John was willing to give up his money for a TV set.

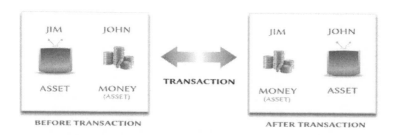

**Money Based Transaction - consummated
No third party involved ("no counterparty risk")**

FIG. 4

On the other hand, currency is issued as debt, and therefore, any transaction based on currency is a transaction based on transferring debt (or promise to pay). In this case, the selling entity gives away goods or services and gets in return from the buyer a central bank's promise to pay. As mentioned before, this is possible only as long as there is a general confidence in the currency.

In this case, the transaction will be finalized only when the seller uses the central bank's promise to buy something else. Still, as long as currency is involved, the party holding the currency will sit with all risks associated with it.

In the next example, Jim has a TV but John has currency, a paper bill—not a real asset, but a promise to pay issued by a central bank. This is good as long as there is enough confidence in the market that the central bank can fulfill its promise. John's currency bill is a risky asset because it depends on the central bank's ability to pay. After the first transaction, John gets an asset (the TV set). He doesn't have any risk anymore, but now Jim is holding the currency bill, and thus Jim has to rely on the central bank's promise. In other words, Jim now holds the risk. The transaction is complete only after Jim has used that currency bill to buy another asset—in this case, an armchair from Mary.

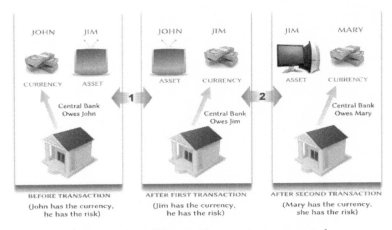

**Currency Based Transaction - not consummated
until currency is used in another transaction
Central bank is involved ("counterparty risk")**   FIG. 5

Jim started with an asset he didn't want (TV set) and finally ended up with an asset he wanted (an armchair). Now he has no counterparty risk. But during the time everybody was using currency bills (promises to pay), it was necessary for Jim to buy another asset in order to consummate a risk-free transaction. At the end, Mary was sitting with the counterparty risk, and this is the case for a paper-money economy. Whoever holds the paper money relies on the ability of the central bank to pay the value of that money (which, as we have seen, is nothing).

Although it seems to be a paradox, the naked truth is that when somebody sells something (goods, services, time, skills) and gets currency in return, they give away something for nothing, but they gladly accept that nothing as payment because they know that the same nothing is good enough to be accepted as payment by somebody else for something else they want or need. Long gone are the days when people needed to barter goods for goods. Modern central banks made it possible to use *nothing* as an acceptable barter medium!

Based on what I have explained so far, here are some basic facts we should always keep in mind.

- Money is neither good nor evil. As long as it is just a reflection of a perceived value, money has no nature or substance in itself—the good or evil is conferred by the actions that money is used for.

- One can also see money as a revealer of a person's true character. A person with a bad character will use money for evil purposes—mainly to acquire power, control other people, and boost ego. All the flaws of a person's character, hard to detect when his or her financial position is modest or average, show up when that person gets lots of money in hand. On the other hand, a person with a good character will always use money to help others and become involved in charitable causes.

- Wealth is about having more than enough of valuable resources and material possessions. Money is a valuable resource as long as it has value in the eyes of others.

- Money in itself provides no form of security—the security is provided by what you can do with it. This is why your search for money is, in fact, a search for protection. Money protects you from the control of others and, by giving you enough flexibility, enables you to control your own decisions.

- Today's money is a currency—this means that it is generated as debt and exists only as long as new debt is generated to pay the applicable interest to earlier generated debt.

In conclusion, you should understand money as nothing but a *tool* that you can use for living your destiny. You are supposed to control money; money is not supposed to control you. In one of his interviews, Scot Anderson, entrepreneur and author of *Think*

Like a Billionaire, Become a Billionaire, said, "People do not live their destiny, because the destiny is not there, but because they become slaves to money. They have to work 40 hours a week to get enough just to get by. Once you build enough to make money work for you, you can do the things you are called to do."

Chapter 5
Wealth as a Mindset

Since childhood, many of us were taught that wealth is the privilege of a few chosen ones—someone else's privilege, and for sure not ours. Unfortunately, for most of us this silly nonsense has stuck with us, and we continue to believe it. As a result, we ended up accepting a life below our true potential, hiding ourselves behind false explanations like cultural background, race, a distressed and dysfunctional family, bad luck—and yes, some of these may indeed be legitimate obstacles that make it harder for some people who are not given much of a chance by society. But still, as I will demonstrate in the following chapters, there are ways to overcome these obstacles.

By studying the lives of wealthy people, you may discover that they have several things in common, regardless of their cultural background and methods they used to build their wealth. Understanding their thinking will give you the chance to start working on your own outlook on yourself and your surroundings and allow you to gain clarity about the changes you need to make in order to build the mindset of a wealthy person. Of course, when you read the principles explained below, you may think of examples of people with a considerable amount of material possessions who do not live according to all of these rules. Still, I will argue that *sound wealth*, wealth that is maintained through economic crises and financial turmoil, is the result of consistent application of these principles.

Understanding Possession and Ownership

Also, I will use the term *possession* rather than *ownership*. Although private ownership is a main pillar of a democratic society, I will argue that wealth is about possessing or having access to material things. As long as our life on this Earth is temporary and no one is buried with his material possessions, the concept of ownership is somehow relative. Even if possessions are passed on from one generation to the next, nobody will ever be able to take his possessions beyond this Earth.

In the following pages, I will review some of the elements that differentiate *wealthy* people from *poverty-minded* people—meaning mainly people who are simply living paycheck to paycheck. These elements represent important indicators for each of us, and you can use them to evaluate your own positions and behaviors. They also represent reminders of what may need to change in your thinking in order for you to develop the wealth mindset.

The Six Areas that Determine a Person's Wealth

Most of us lack any form of financial education; our school systems do not provide it and families do not do a good job either. Honestly, we are quick to blame our parents for not teaching us better, but we forget that they didn't know much about it themselves in the first place. This is why, when it comes to money, we just put everything in one basket—we call it personal finances, and because we think that it's too hard to understand, we just leave everything in the hands of others—financial planners, advisers, consultants. While these people have their role and good advice is indeed valuable, the truth is that we are much better positioned to take the right decisions when we gain more insight into these matters.

It is impossible to build wealth without a clear knowledge of the structure of personal finances. This is why, in this chapter, I will focus on the six areas that belong to the generic concept of personal finances and that any person needs to keep under close observation.

These areas are:

1. Income

2. Expenses

3. Savings

4. Investments

5. Debt and leverage

6. Insurance

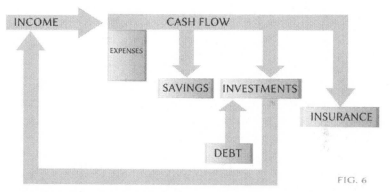

FIG. 6

Figure 6 depicts these distinct areas. Each of them serves a purpose, and understanding both purpose and the healthy principles applicable for each area will determine whether you will manage to build wealth—or not. In the following pages, I will examine each of them.

Income

Your income is your most important tool for wealth building. Regardless if it's your paycheck from a place of employment, an income from running your own business, or a return on an earlier investment—all these represent an inflow of money that can be used in two directions:

- to cover your living expenses;

- to provide resources for savings, investment, and insurance.

So, the purpose of your income is to cover your living expenses and to provide additional resources for savings, investments, and insurance.

How do wealthy people relate to their income? They are always in search of finding ways to increase their income, and this is mainly done in two ways:

- generating multiple streams of income;

- increasing the income from each individual stream.

This is not about being greedy, although greed can be in itself an important motivator in searching for more money (as I will advocate in a later section of this book, true wealth goes hand in hand with generosity). But there are several reasons why you should look to develop several streams of income.

First of all, *living within your means is essential for building wealth.* Consumer debt is not a solution, as this will keep you broke and grab ahold of most of your future income. If you want a better life, you need to constantly expand your means, because there is always a limit on what you can do by cutting expenses. For instance, you can spend less on food by going the junk food route, eating cheap products filled with artificial additives and chemical ingredients. In the longer run, however, you risk chronic disease and ending up with high medical expenses. In conclusion, while you make sure that you do not spend more than you make, you need to make more in order to have a better life.

Another reason to create several streams of income is that it gives you *more flexibility in case you are forced to sell some assets.* If you don't get an acceptable price, you can wait because the other streams sustain you. If you are forced to sell, you are in a cornered position and have to accept the buyer's conditions.

Also, you need several streams of income because you, like everybody else, *live in an inflationary environment*. When governments and central banks have a declared goal of inflating the money supply, they create an environment where money loses purchasing power. As time goes by, you need more money just to maintain your living standard, and you have no guarantee that your single source of income will keep up with price increases generated by inflation.

But maybe the most important reason to look for multiple streams of income is that *this will reduce vulnerability in case something goes wrong*. If you live paycheck to paycheck, and that paycheck is your only source of income, you are totally dependent on your employer. If your job disappears, so does your income. If you run a business and one single customer provides most of the revenues, you are equally vulnerable.

There are several ways to generate multiple streams of income, and the most common mistake is to ignore simple methods of generating extra cash just because they would bring only small amounts. These methods can vary from taking additional part-time assignments, running a small home-based business, investing in real estate or other income-generating assets, providing different services, or even converting a hobby into a small business. In developing your income base, there are some important things to consider.

Become an Expert

Regardless of the industry or area they are active in, people who decide to build wealth focus first on identifying a business model or method that suits them best. This may require some trial and error before finding the best model and also some adaptation along the way. But then, when the model works, they will repeat the same method or model in different deals, perfecting it as they go and learning at the same time the pitfalls and challenges associated with that method. This will enable them to master it, have full control in every moment, and successfully repeat it in different transactions.

In his book Creating Wealth: Retire in Ten Years Using Allen's Seven Principles of Wealth, Robert Allen introduces the "cookie-cutter" concept. He says, "A cookie cutter is a formula, a method that successful investors use over and over again to cut dough out of their particular investment marketplace. They are experts in their chosen fields. They adapt their personalities to the circumstances and they use these cookie cutters repeatedly" (p. 84).

In this particular case, he makes reference to several different methods of doing transactions in real estate. Some people focus on buying houses and flipping them to sell after a short while for a profit. Others, especially those who have the skills to do some work themselves, prefer to buy run-down houses, fix them up, and resell them for a profit. Some may prefer to buy a house in good condition and rent it out, while others may want to fix the house up and keep it as a rental. In developing your own cookie-cutter business concept, what matters is identifying that particular method that suits you best and perfecting it while getting involved in similar transactions again and again.

Have a Clear Vision and a Long-Term Plan

Wealth is based on long-term vision, a vision that in many cases will span several generations. Vision is one of the cornerstones of a life of abundance. External factors and circumstances may always change, but the vision remains the guiding light that leads to the future, regardless of impending storms. Charles Noble said, "You must have long-range goals to keep you from being frustrated by short-range failures." External factors and circumstances may add a lot of noise and even lead to detours, but should never affect the final destination.

The concept of vision is not something mystical or highly spiritual. It is something we carry in our hearts, on the inside of us, and we can move toward it based on our abilities, skills, and strengths. Vision is not something static either—it needs redefining and adjusting every now and then, depending on the external factors with which one has to operate. A businessperson needs to take into consideration the changing environment in which his or her business will operate.

People who build wealth over time have a clear vision for their life—they know what their purpose is and which direction to follow. Also, they work hard to fulfill that vision. They develop a strategy of how to achieve the vision, and they see hard work as the only legitimate source of wealth. They may be in businesses seen as speculative—for example, the stock market, commodities, the FOREX exchange. Still, they dedicate a significant amount of time, on a constant basis, to understanding how these markets operate.

See Yourself Wealthy before You Become Wealthy

Wealthy people know they are destined for greatness. This may sound like a nice cliché, but you need to have an image in your mind that will cause you to rise up to the challenges you'll face as a wealthy person. Otherwise, you will not move ahead, or if you somehow make it to the level of being wealthy, you will have a hard time maintaining your position.

You may be tempted to think about wealth as a provider of rights and privileges, but you should not forget that it also comes with responsibilities, obligations, and duties. This is why seeing yourself in a wealthy position does not mean *faking* to get there. Seeing yourself as a multimillionaire does not mean *pretending* to be one—for instance, wearing a cheap Rolex replica and expecting to be noticed at some vanity event. Focusing on the image, on external glamour elements, is nothing more than seeking approval and acceptance.

Seeing yourself wealthy means concentrating on your internal strengths, on your differentiators, what makes you an original, and how you can turn all these particularities, with hard work, into *assets* that are *valuable* in the marketplace. When you are able to offer value in the marketplace, people will surely return its worth.

Seeing yourself wealthy also means also developing the good habits of wealthy people early on, before becoming wealthy. Believing that money or material things will solve your problems is one of the biggest lies you can ever believe. You need to change your thinking and mentality *before* possessing the money, because it is not the money that creates your world, it is your thinking and mentality.

Let us think for a minute what happens when somebody buys a new car. The old car was dirty and filled with junk. What happens in a matter of weeks? The nice and smelling-like-new car turns into a replica of the old one—newer, but still filled with junk. The same applies to the house. A person who lives in a messy one-bedroom apartment may think that keeping a mansion in order is easier just because it has more storage space and there is always a maid around cleaning up the mess. Still, maids and helpers are there to execute what the owners require, and if the owners do not know what to require, maids and helpers will be confused, not knowing what is expected from them, and will not perform. With all available help, the mansion will still be a mess. In other words, even if you make a decision to become wealthy, your belief system will pull you down to your level of complacency. It may not be what you want, but it's the level where everything is comfortable.

This is why is important to change your thinking and belief system and leave your comfort zone; this is the only thing that will generate enough motivation for you to move on. Unfortunately, too many people get comfortable and complacent in their poverty. Neale Donald Walsch, the author of *Conversations with God*, once wrote, "Your life begins at the end of your comfort zone." In many cases, rejecting the idea of poverty has proved to be a good motivator, as it did for Tyler Perry. When talking about his success, he stated in an interview,

> I've been often asked why I work as hard as I do. In the beginning, part of it was that I was running away from poverty. The first 20 years of my life were pretty dismal and I never wanted to experience that kind of life again. It was such a dismal horrible place that no amount of work would get me far enough away from it.

Do Not Take Shortcuts, Because the Difference Will Always Have to Be Paid!

Lack of patience will cause you to look for shortcuts to reach your goals faster, believing that this means increased efficiency. A shortcut is good as long as it is about eliminating unnecessary steps. But when a shortcut is about skipping steps, it will prove to be a bad choice. In fact, all great achievements are the result of a step-by-step approach, where each step is taken on a foundation built from earlier steps. The pressure in society to perform faster and better may lead you into temptation to take steps without building such a foundation.

In private life, taking a shortcut could mean jumping into a committed relationship without knowing everything you need to know about the person you commit to and hoping to make things work in time. In business, this means to rush expanding a business before the business model is fine-tuned, hoping that economy-of-scale benefits will compensate for flaws in the management system. It may also mean entering into partnerships with people who have different agendas in order to expedite the development process of a business. There is always a cost associated with unnecessary delays; therefore, procrastinating is not a good solution. The fact is, when taking a shortcut, you will always end up paying the difference.

Compromising to Get Something Will Require Future Compromising to Keep It.

Compromise is very often seen as a necessary evil. There are different ways to define compromise, many of them used to justify its necessity. I prefer to see a compromise as "the acceptance of conditions or terms that contradict a person's own values and convictions."

Negotiations and win-win situations are never the result of compromises. In a compromise, the person accepting terms that contradict their own core values will never be happy with the result because of the feeling that they gave too much and received too little. And the fact is that compromise does not stop there, upon getting something. After getting it, the only way to keep the thing is to continue to compromise in the same manner. In itself, a compromise is unfair. Therefore, all efforts to keep the result of a compromise will not restore fairness.

Value Integrity

Many voices claim that there is hardly any honest way to build wealth without cheating, lying, and scheming. The truth is that long-lasting wealth cannot be built on any other foundation than honesty and integrity. There are of course examples of people who became very rich (have lots of money) or accumulated huge amounts of assets using shameful methods, but in most cases, these do not last too long. The wickedness is soon to be discovered and everything vanishes in no time.

The principle of "sowing and reaping" works in both directions, not just for the good. Use of despicable methods of business where the focus is solely personal short-term gain will seriously backfire. For instance, one of the greatest temptations for business owners is to go beyond the edge of the law in order to cut taxes. The idea behind it is very logical: we pay enough taxes anyway—why not find some ways to pay less?

There are industries where this temptation is harder to resist because of the nature of the business, such as the food service industry, a business that I personally know pretty well. According to www.restaurant.org, there are 980,000 restaurant locations in the US alone, with total sales revenues of $660 billion per year, making it one of the most important industries in the country. Since there are many cash transactions in this business, there is always a seductive attraction to circumvent the reporting system and pocket some of the money directly. Beyond the legal implications and risks, this strategy will prove to provide only short-term benefits, because every method implemented by management to circumvent the system and hide revenues will open additional doors for employees to take their share by hiding revenues from the management. Unfortunately, the losses generated by unfaithful employees may exceed several times the "tax savings" generated by these practices.

Integrity is one of the greatest personal assets, and the same can be said about honest business practices.

Expenses

Out of the six areas of personal finances, *expenses* is probably the one that needs almost no introduction. We all face them every day—when we pick up our mail from the mailbox, most of the envelopes contain bills to pay. And unfortunately, this is the area that causes most trouble for our personal finances. In order to understand why, we need to recall a statement I made when I described *income*. I said that income's purpose is to (1) cover our living expenses and (2) allow for savings, investments, and insurance. The direct consequence of this fact is that *income has to exceed expenses* in order to accommodate funding of the other areas of personal finances. Turning this around, *our living expenses have to be lower than our income.* This is nothing else but the old common-sense wisdom about "living within your means."

Living within your means is the same as *living on a budget* — a concept that for most people has a negative connotation, because they see it as about cutting all indulgences. But living on a budget is not about constraints, it is about you deciding the destinations of your money instead of letting your money flow out at any impulse. In other words, it is about you mastering your money or the money mastering you. Having a budget is nothing but a plan about your expenses. Larry Winget, "The Pitbull of Personal Development©" and author of several best sellers, including *You're Broke Because You Want to Be*, says, "Nobody ever wrote a plan to be broke. Broke happens when you don't have a plan."

The purpose of expense planning is to offer you a living standard according to your personal goals, aspirations, and desires. With that in mind, let us see some of the common traits of wealthy people when it comes to their spending behavior.

Hate Waste While Still Being Generous

Building wealth is about accumulating valuable possessions. Accumulation and waste exclude each other. Wealthy people eliminate any kind of waste in their life. They are not cheap or stingy, because they value themselves and treat themselves right, including their families. They value all the resources they have available—assets, contact networks, time, ideas, know-how, opportunities—and they never waste them.

Wealthy people have the ability to draw the line between wasting and spending. They clearly define what their needs are, and they are not easily moved beyond the definition, regardless of whether the needs are their own or someone else's. They know that emotions can lead to hasty decisions, and therefore they develop or join systems supporting different forms of charities. All their "Good Samaritan" actions are taken care of in an organized manner and not subject to impulse or external pressure and manipulations.

Prudence does not eliminate generosity in a wealthy person's life. However, being focused on maximizing the use of available resources will yield possibilities for generosity in areas that align with their values and philanthropic areas of interest. This mechanism is very simple. Reduced or even eliminated waste will free resources that can be used for being generous with family and friends, or with church, charity, political, or social organizations. In fact, the generosity becomes much more efficient through savings generated in the process of eliminating waste.

We hear all too often the opinion that "it's just fair and right if wealthy people give back to society." This opinion implies that the wealth was somehow fraudulently taken from society, and, as compensation, something should be given back. However, the main reason wealthy people are generous is that they understand the universal principle of "sowing and reaping." This is not necessarily a principle that works like an investment account, where you put some money into it and expect something back in the same form in which it was sown. Wealthy people are generous because they understand that they live a life of abundance and want to share their wealth, not because they feel guilty for having too much.

Guilt is never a good motivator in any situation or circumstance. Being generous with others in mind will allow one to harvest more. "Give and it shall be given back to you" is not about using God as leverage; it is about stretching a helping hand and not thinking about the reward. The reward is just a consequence, not the motivation. Describing her involvement in charitable work, J. K. Rowling, the successful author of the Harry Potter series, said on the TV documentary J. K. Rowling: A Year in the Life: "Initially, I wasn't very organized with my giving. I didn't have a thought-through system. And, again, that was becoming a bit overwhelming as well. So I have a charitable trust now, and we've refined the objectives of the trust, which was a very useful exercise."

Be Frugal, but Not Cheap (or Understand the Difference between Price and Value)

Very rarely do wealthy people fall into a pattern of "impulse buying" or "emotional shopping." In order to make a good decision when making a purchase, they tend to carefully weigh and assess the importance, necessity, and value-added nature of their purchases, especially those that can potentially yield a profit. They also know that high-quality merchandise is built to last and is worth paying for. They never buy cheap goods that can be used just a few times before they inevitably fall apart.

Being "frugal" is not the same as being "cheap". Being frugal means to understand "value"—that is, deciding for the long-term benefit of a purchase and then finding the best deal available. Sometimes, if situation allows for it, it may also mean postponing the purchase until a good deal shows up. On the other hand, being cheap is about focusing only on the price tag. A cheap person will always disregard the long-term benefit of a purchase and choose the lowest price.

There is a saying that "there is nothing more expensive than cheap things." We all have experienced emergency situations when we hastily bought something that was poorly made and designed (basically . . . cheap), only to discover that the thing falls apart almost immediately. Years ago when visiting New York, I was caught in an unexpected heavy rain. The solution was pretty obvious, or at least I thought so—find something inexpensive that would at least get me through the evening, so I bought a $5 umbrella in the subway station. It disintegrated after only five wind blasts. At a price of $1 per wind blast, that was indeed a bad deal for me. This was an example of merely "patching," where we end up having to pay a higher price for a real, long-term solution.

Understand the Power of Compound Growth (Cash Flow Accumulation)

There is a common propensity to ignore the small amounts paid on small things when purchasing items that we do not necessarily need. The basic thinking behind this is that "you can't do much with a few bucks anyway." While indeed there is not much you can do with a few bucks, if those few bucks are spent regularly, the difference is significant. Those few bucks can come from

- bad habits or habits that add no value to our life—like smoking and excess drinking;

- impulse shopping;

- convenience shopping—buying in small quantities things that we use a lot, while we could save a lot by buying the same things in bulk.

David Bach, author of several bestsellers (The Automatic Millionaire, The Automatic Millionaire Homeowner; Start Late, Finish Rich; Smart Women Finish Rich; Debt Free for Life) introduced a concept called "The Latte Factor©," pointing out in his book The Automatic Millionaire Homeowner: "We've all got more money than we think. The problem is that we often waste it on small things that we want but don't really need." As he explains it, "We can save ourselves a fortune, maybe a down payment for a house, if we just start keeping track of where it goes and holding on to some of it."

In order to have a clearer understanding of this difference, let's look at it a bit closer over a time period of 10 years:

- spending $5 every day on small things, or

- saving $5 daily and investing it on a quarterly basis, with a return of 5 percent per year.

The figures are astonishing. In 10 years, the total amount spent is $18,250. If the same $5 is saved daily and invested with 5 percent annual return, the total amount is $23,170. So, just $5 per day means, in 10 years, a difference of $41,420. Instead of having a loss of over $18,000, you can have an asset of over $23,000. You can gain all this just by eliminating unnecessary spending on small things that do not benefit you in the long run.

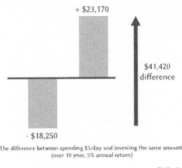

+ $23,170

$41,420 difference

- $18,250

The difference between spending $5/day and investing the same amount.
(over 10 year, 5% annual return)

FIG. 7

You have to understand that this is not about things like depriving yourself of your favorite coffee brand. After all, you can buy the coffee you love at the supermarket (be it Starbucks, Caribou, or Dunkin' Donuts, to name just a few) and brew it at home for less than 50¢ per cup. You are indeed deprived of the experience of standing in line, getting it mixed by the barista, and being seen with the "right" cup in your hand, and you may even argue that it is not the same taste. But the point here is not about being a cheapskate who deprives yourself of your favorite beverage, but about whether you are willing to give up the coffee store experience for a while in order to build up the means you need to invest so you can later use the returns of the investment to have an even better latte experience. It is like giving up the $3 latte now so you can fully enjoy the $6 latte later on.

With reference to bulk purchases of goods that we use in large quantities, the savings are in the range of 20 to 50 percent, sometimes even more. You may think that it's better to buy in small quantities in order to not affect the monthly cash flow and maybe invest the difference. A while ago, I was driven by the same philosophy. After doing the math, I found out that there is hardly any legitimate investment that makes the same level of return as the discounts provided by buying bulk. Simply, you have to look at the extra money you pay for a larger quantity as an initial investment and consider every saving as you use the product as a return on that investment. Many types of products can be purchased in bulk, with large discounts; while it doesn't necessarily make sense to purchase a two-year supply of ketchup and mustard, everything that has a long shelf life and can be stored at room temperature does qualify for this kind of purchase: hygiene products and toiletries (soap, toilet paper, toothpaste, razor blades, diapers, pads); kitchen consumables (dishwasher soap, paper towels, aluminum foil, wrapping foil); long-lasting food (rice, canned food, pasta, cereals, oils); and other consumables (batteries, light bulbs). Bulk purchasing should be considered a high-priority investment because, in addition to the high return, it is also risk free—you are buying things you are going to use anyway.

Another important illustration of the impact of small payments is making additional monthly payments for paying down a mortgage. Here I will use the Early Payoff Calculator provided by Dave Ramsey on his web page *www.daveramsey.com*. Let us assume that you decide to buy a $250,000 house, of which $50,000 is down payment and the balance of $200,000 is financed with a 5 percent fixed-rate 30-year mortgage. The numbers speak for themselves. If you choose to follow the bank's regular schedule, the monthly payment would be $1,073.64. The total amount paid during the 30 years is $386,513.24, of which $186,513.24 represents interest.

Assuming that you decide to pay an extra $100 per month against the principal, this alone will reduce the mortgage payback time from 30 years to 24 years and 11 months. So, expressed in time units, the duration of the loan is reduced by 5 years and 1 month. Expressed in money saved, we are talking about $36,825.85. The total amount you will pay in this case is $349,687.39, of which $149,687.39 represents interest.

In conclusion, the additional extra effort of saving just over $3 per day (which is equivalent to $100 per month) will give you and your family the chance to save $36,825.85 in interest and be debt free 5 years earlier. This means that, for more than 5 years, you will be able to keep the $1,073.64 you would normally pay to the bank every month.

Now, if we repeat the same exercise but presume that you want to stretch the effort even further and double the amount, that would mean paying an extra $200 every month. The results are even more spectacular. The loan duration is reduced by 8 years and 8 months, and the total interest savings are $60,784.03.

In conclusion, all these examples illustrate the power of cash flow accumulation. It is not about depriving yourself of the small pleasures of life (nothing wrong in treating ourselves occasionally), but rather understanding the financial impact of your patterns of convenience.

This also illustrates that, applied to compound growth principles, *time* represents either your greatest enemy when you are in debt (negative cash flow accumulation), or your greatest ally when you save and invest (positive cash flow accumulation).

Develop the Ability to Find Bargains

In time, wealthy people develop the ability to find bargains. This works in two ways: on one hand, they are constantly looking for good deals, and if good deals do not show up, they wait patiently. This is a practice developed through years, and as time goes by, they become better at identifying opportunities for good deals. They do not necessarily rush into a deal just to conclude it. On the other hand, they have built a reputation of being reasonable buyers, so people who are in a rush to sell something will search for such people first before they take their product out on the market. A buyer who is not forced to buy facing a seller forced to sell is in a very advantageous position, and although he does not necessarily adopt a take-it-or-leave it attitude, he will still ensure a good deal.

Prefer to Invest First and Spend After

As I have mentioned before, wealthy people do not waste, they spend wisely, making sure that they get a fair benefit out of the resources they release. In addition, they limit or even postpone spending, preferring to invest the resources they have available in assets with intrinsic and underlying value that generate a flow of return over a long period of time. The purpose is to build up a volume of assets that generates a flow of future returns; these future revenue streams can be used later on for spending, without decreasing the value of those assets. For instance, instead of spending money every few years buying an expensive new car, wealthy people keep driving the same older car for several years and invest the money that could be used for purchasing a new car right away in assets that will generate returns that will pay for purchasing a new car later on.

This method can be referred to as the "bucket principle." Instead of letting cash flow out right away after acquiring it, a part of these resources are directed to be accumulated into a portfolio of investments (the bucket) that will soon generate a return. The process continues, including also reinvesting the return, until "the bucket is filled up" and creates overflow. This means that the investment portfolio has reached a value where, even if the return percentage is low, the total amount returned will give enough to make a good living. For example, based on an average return of 5 percent, an investment portfolio of $2,000,000 will be able to generate $100,000 per year in revenues. If the investment vehicles are carefully monitored ensuring this kind of return, the $100,000 represents an overflow that can be spent without affecting the $2,000,000 portfolio.

This also means that wealthy people are always aware of their financial situation—both in terms of assets and liabilities. Statistics show that most poor people do not have a full overview of their financial standing, meaning they do not know how much they owe and to whom they owe it. As a consequence, they do not make any attempt to reduce their debt or control their expenses. Jean Chatzky, financial journalist, speaker, and author, explains in her book Pay It Down—From Debt to Wealth in $10 a Day, "Not knowing how much you owe, to whom and at what interest rate allows you to spend as if the problem doesn't exist" (p. 11).

Resist Poverty Mindset, Because Being Poor Always Costs More

Wealthy people are always considered a low-risk category for banks and financial institutions. They are always attractive as customers for these entities, and therefore, banks stretch long and do go the extra mile to gain and keep them as customers. They maintain a high credit rating, and although they use leverage (using banks' money for investments), they get very good conditions and low interest. Banks are happy to deal with them because any borrower's liability is an asset for the bank.

Wealthy people always keep their credits and liabilities within reasonable limits, making sure that these limits are not exceeded. They use credit cards just for convenience and not because they need the money; this is why they fully pay all bills before their due date, taking advantage of the interest-free period.

Wealthy people never pay late fees, reminder fees, or any form of penalties for delayed payments. In real estate, all landlords apply a late fee if rent is paid later than a certain date. Paying a late fee of $50 every month for a $1,000 rent, a tenant will give to the landlord an additional cash flow of $600 per year—a return that, in some cases, may be similar to or even higher than the cash flow generated by that property.

On the other hand, people considered high risk have to pay a high price for "being poor." They have to buy everything on credit, and because of higher interest rates, they end up paying double for everything. In addition, they pay all kinds of penalties and provisions for delayed payments—charges that are always paid before any other obligations (interest and principal).

In order to illustrate the difference between great and bad credit ratings, I can make reference to a couple of examples. Let us suppose that someone wants to purchase a $20,000 car and finance it with a 5-year loan. A great credit score would allow somebody to finance the purchase at approximately a 3 percent interest rate—meaning overall interest costs of $1,550. A person with a bad credit rating would get the same loan paying around 10 percent interest, leading to overall interest costs of approximately $5,500. So the difference, paid over 5 years, is $4,000.

You may argue that a $20,000 car is only a "nice to have" item, and therefore the example is not fully relevant. So, let us see how things roll out in case of a $250,000 home loan. A home is a must-have. A great credit rating gives access to an interest rate of 3.8 percent for a 30-year mortgage. The overall interest costs, paid over the entire period, would be $170,000—representing approximately 68 percent of the value of the house. On the other hand, an applicant with a bad credit score (in case he is still approved by the lenders) may be asked to pay around 6.5 percent for the same house. In this case, the overall interest costs, paid over the entire 30-year period, would be $318,870—representing 127 percent of the house value.

Of course, you can say that interest rates vary through time, which is true. Still, the interest rate will always depend on the applicant's credit rating, and a 3 percent spread between a great and a bad rating is expected to apply at all times. The important lesson to be learned from this example is that a borrower with bad credit will pay interest costs that are almost double those paid by a borrower with great credit. In other words, it doesn't "pay to be poor," as this makes one pay just in interest much more than the value of the entire house.

Savings

Savings, the third area of personal finances, is also commonly understood and apparently intuitive. Old sayings like "save for a rainy day" are familiar to everyone. Still, there may be some confusion and misunderstanding, as there is a thin borderline between *savings* and *investments*. Many people consider them to belong to the same category, but as I will show below, they serve different purposes.

The main purpose of savings is *protection*—that is, to possess a buffer of cash (or other liquid assets that can easily be converted into cash) that can cover for one's expenses for a limited period of time. As long as the purpose of saving is protection, the focus of a savings portfolio is *safety* and *preserving value*. Further, that means assuming minimal risks. This is completely different from the purpose of investments, which, as we will see in the next section, is to provide return. Because there is a direct correlation between returns and risk, an investment portfolio is always structured on riskier assets.

Considering savings and investments in the same category creates an important disadvantage because this kind of thinking will always try to find a balance between safety and expectations for return. While attempting to achieve the right balance (or "a little bit of both"), the end result may be "nothing of anything." In other words, a strategy to get a reasonable return with a reasonable risk may lead to an allocation that, seen from a savings perspective, is too risky, and seen from an investment perspective, is not providing sufficient return.

Saving money makes sense as long as money represents a store of value. Saving currency (beyond a reasonable level, necessary for protection) makes no sense because there is no intrinsic value; currency produces effects only when it flows and changes hands.

So, savings should be available to cover our living expenses if some unexpected and undesirable event occurs—job loss, accident, sickness. We have all gone through some times of trouble of some sort, and we know that just turning a difficult situation around requires lots of personal resources—not only material, but also psychological. The last thing we need is additional pressure and worries tied to financial struggles.

In some cases, like a job loss, replacing a part of the income may not be so difficult. Taking any other job, even below one's qualifications and lower paid, will most probably avoid dramatic situations like defaulting on mortgage payments or utilities or not having enough money for food. But in some other situations, like sickness or any other situation when working is not possible, finding alternative income is not an option. In such circumstances, savings remove the pressure of generating income to cover for expenses and give us the necessary room to focus on solutions to the problems we face.

Defining the appropriate saving strategy is not as easy, and raises two main questions. The first one is: How do we save and what are the best means to use for savings? The second is: How much we are supposed to save? In order for saving to serve its purpose (protection for difficult times), our savings must be first of all very liquid. This is necessary because, when emergencies occur, we need money fast. Cash and bank accounts are definitely the most liquid forms of savings. Other liquid options include CDs (certificates of deposit) and money market funds.

But keeping money in a bank account creates two disadvantages. The first one is related to the very low interest rate paid by banks for deposits. In fact, the real interest rates are negative if we factor in inflation. That means that keeping money in a savings account leads to a loss, as money loses its purchasing power. The second disadvantage is that, in legal terms, *when we deposit money in the bank, that money is not ours anymore—it represents a loan we give to the bank*. Of course, the bank has the legal obligation to pay us any amount we require out of our account, but as long as we deposit money, the bank can do with it whatever it desires. We, depositors, become simply creditors to the bank.

Other forms of paper assets, like publicly listed stocks, bonds, or shares in mutual funds, may provide a higher return, compensating for inflation. But these are speculative assets and extremely volatile (meaning that their prices can increase or decrease significantly in the short term).

In the end, it is all a matter of personal choice. Some people prefer to keep the cash in their accounts and willingly accept the depreciation; they consider the loss to be an insurance premium— something to be paid in order to be assured that, if something bad occurs, they have the means to avoid disaster. Some people prefer to take that higher risk and try to minimize risk by diversifying into different financial products.

With regard to how much we should have as savings, there are different opinions. The range is from 3 months to 12 months, with most authors recommending an equivalent of 6 months' expenses. That means that the amount you should have as your savings should be high enough to cover your living expenses, without affecting your living standard, for a period of 6 months. In other words, it should cover necessities (home mortgage or rent, car payments, utilities, gas, transportation, insurance, food, some basic clothing), but also allow for some discretionary spending. Of course, a difficult period requires some adjustments—for instance, cooking at home instead of dining out, or renting a movie instead of going to the theater. Maybe even more drastic measures, like selling the second car, may be necessary. Anyway, in order to make the situation more bearable and avoid all negative psychological impact, a significant change in lifestyle is not desirable.

Should our savings cover *more* than six months of living? This is an individual choice—how much you need to have a feeling of safety. The reason for setting a limit of six months is that it is assumed that any event that affects your ability to generate income for a period longer than six months is covered by one or another form of insurance (something that we will elaborate upon a bit further, when we discuss insurance). Another reason why saving beyond six months of living is not necessary is the nature of money itself. As I said in Chapter 4, today's currencies are not real assets, but rather *debt*—promises to pay issued by a central bank. That means that when you save in a certain currency, you don't accumulate real assets, you accumulate someone else's debt. Sure, that "someone else" is a central bank, and unlike any other debtor, it has the full backing of the government; still, it's not a real asset, it's someone else's promise to pay.

"Saving for Retirement" or "Investing for Retirement"?

I can't stress enough how important it is to have savings that protect you in case of unexpected events. Still, there is one thing that I consider to be somehow misunderstood and can even be considered a trap—the concept of saving for retirement. The idea is that you should set aside a part of your income during your working career and accumulate a significant amount until you retire. After retirement, as your income is expected to be lower than your expenses, you take out periodically (consume) small chunks of this amount. And, if you have accumulated enough, you will be able to have a decent living during the last part of your life. Although planning for retirement is correct thinking, there are some challenges with considering this as saving.

First of all, if the purpose of saving is seen as protection against unexpected events, as I defined it earlier, saving is not the right tool. Retirement is not an unexpected event. Everybody gets older, and at some point in life, will retire. Some may want to do it earlier; some may want to do it later. Retirement is not only expected, but is something that many look forward to.

Second, saving is about lost value. The concept of saving for retirement may work better in an environment where preservation of purchasing power over time is guaranteed. But, as I mentioned when I clarified the difference between money and currency, all our existing currencies are constantly losing their purchasing power. If we take into consideration an inflation rate of 2 percent per year (which central banks define today as "ideal" or their "target") and a time horizon of 40 years between the moment a certain amount is deposited in a savings account and the moment the same amount is withdrawn to be spent, we are talking about at least an 80 percent loss of purchasing power, without taking into account the compound effect. In other words, if somebody makes a deposit of $1,000 at the age of 30 and takes his money out at the age of 70, he will be able to buy just 20 percent of the goods he would have been able to buy at the age of 30. The interest rates for bank deposits are significantly below inflation (currently in the US way below 1 percent, and in Europe banks even introduced nominal negative interest rates), so there is no real compensation for this loss.

The third problem with saving is about *spending the principal*. According to Kevin O'Leary, a very important principle of wealth building is "spend the return, never the principal." The idea of spending money accumulated in earlier years also totally contradicts the "bucket principle" as I described it when I talked about expenses—resources directed to be accumulated into a portfolio of investments ("the bucket") that generates sufficient return ("overflow").

In conclusion, planning for retirement by saving now and spending later is a bad concept. The correct concept is to keep the savings separate, with the only purpose being protection during difficult times. When it comes to planning for retirement, the correct option is to *invest* for it—and this is what we will take a closer look at in the next section of this chapter.

Investments

As one of the most discussed and debated areas related to finances, investments should represent a high priority for each individual. This is an area where you can find an evident mix of simplicity and complexity. Despite the fact that history identifies people who managed to build and maintain great wealth by consistently applying a few simple rules, most people consider investments to be very complex and sophisticated and should, therefore, be entirely outsourced to financial planners and advisers. There are indeed many advanced financial products on the market, and the Internet has made them available for anybody. This is why it's easy to mistake *availability* for *simplicity*, which is not the case. After all, understanding the fields you are investing in is the key to avoiding costly mistakes.

Different from savings, where the purpose is to protect, the purpose of investments is to *build wealth by providing return and cash flow*. In Chapter 3, I described investment as being "release of a resource with the purpose of providing a return." The principle is very simple: something of value in our possession is released out into the marketplace, and this produces a future stream of returns while maintaining the initial value. This idea can be found expressed in many ways in articles, books, and other materials—for instance, Jerry Robinson, host of the *FTM Daily Show* (www.ftmdaily.com) and author of the best seller *Bankruptcy of Our Nation*, expresses it as "to trade cash for cash flow."

As this is not a book about financial investments in particular, we will just review some of the most important areas where we can make investments. Although references are made to some absolutely necessary technical aspects, I will rather adopt a common-sense outlook, trying to highlight the advantages, challenges, and particularities of each area. In other words, I would like to focus on those aspects that allow us to take advantage of the simplicity factor, where we can still understand the underlying elements of each investment vehicle. The most common areas for individual investors are the following:

- Owning a business

- Stocks / shares in other companies

- Bonds

- Mutual funds

- Real estate

- Precious metals

Owning a Business

This is the most usual form of investment for any individual, and, in most cases, more accessible than we think. And when we talk about owning your own business, we do not necessarily mean that you have to own a business that gives you enough income to make enough living to replace your current employment. As we discussed when I talked about generating multiple streams of income, many small business types can be started at home without significant investment. Some businesses require only time; others require both time and some money. A business that has no or minimal fixed costs will be able to generate a constant stream of income every month, even in the start phase, when sales are low. In time, as a business grows, one can make a decision whether to expand the business or not.

Individual Stocks

A stock represents a share of a corporation's capital. In other words, when you purchase one stock of a big corporation, you come into possession of "one slice" of the corporation. How big is your slice? Depends on the total number of available shares, and how many shares you own. If a corporation has 1,000 stocks and you own one stock, you have a share of 1/1,000 of the company's assets. If the corporation has one million stocks and you own one stock, you have a share of 1/1,000,000 of the company's assets. Each stock gives you the right to a share of corporation's profits. Simply put, when a corporation makes $1,000,000 profit per year and you own one of the one million stocks of that corporation, your profit share is $1. In practice, this does not mean that this amount is transferred directly to your bank account—because the corporation will use some of that profit for different purposes.

Further, the stock price is based on a multiplier of the profits called the "Price/Earnings Ratio" (or P/E). This is one of the most important indicators used by financial analysts. Based on the example above, if a company makes a profit per share of $1, and one stock (share) is priced at $10, the company has a P/E of 10. If the stock price is $15, then the P/E is 15.

Investing in stocks generates returns in two ways:

- dividends (a share of the profit, paid periodically—monthly or quarterly);

- stock price appreciation.

Dividends are the amounts paid to investors as a share of the profits. *Stock price appreciation* occurs when the price of the stock increases. Investing in stocks is considered to be risky because, in case the corporation goes into bankruptcy, the stockholders are the last to be paid. If a company is declared bankrupt, an appointed liquidator will sell the company's assets on the open market, trying to get the best prices. These are normally way lower than the real value of the assets, aka "pennies on the dollar." Then, out of the collected funds, the liquidator will pay all outstanding obligations of the company and all costs related to the bankruptcy and liquidation process. Finally, and only if there are any funds left, are these distributed to shareholders.

Exchange Listed or Privately Held?

As an investor, you can buy stocks in publicly listed corporations (on the stock exchange) or privately held corporations. Stocks listed on a stock exchange have the advantage that they are very liquid— meaning that, if you want to sell some stocks, there are always some buyers out there. If the stock prices are falling, you may not get the price you like, and you may even need to take a loss. But at least you can sell your stocks and get cash in a short time. On the other hand, you should be aware of some challenges related to pricing of publicly listed stocks.

First, investment is about *stock prices*. Traditionally, stock prices have been calculated based on expectations of the corporation's ability to generate profit in the long term (the so-called *fundamentals*). The key word here is not *profit* and not even *ability* (although a corporation's ability to generate profit is one of the fundamental elements in stock investing); the key word is *expectations*. If investors assume that "fundamentals are strong," meaning that the corporation has what it takes (right products, strategy, resources, etc.) to generate increasing profits, they are willing to buy stocks and pay higher prices for them. If investors assume that "fundamentals are weak," meaning that prospects to generate profits are not good, they will dump stocks on the market, even though they may register a loss. The idea of limiting the loss *now* is more attractive than risking greater losses while waiting for later gains.

Because stock prices are tied to *expectations*, they fluctuate significantly due to these shifting expectations—a phenomenon in the stock market called *volatility*. As most experts point out, *greed* and *fear* are the two most important feelings involved in creating this volatility. Figure 8 illustrates a classic bubble wave. In the first phase, called "the smart money phase" by Grant Williams, portfolio and strategy adviser to Vulpes Investment Management in Singapore, author of the financial newsletter *Things That Make You Go Hmmm...* (www.ttmygh.com) and founder of *Real Vision TV* (realvisiontv.com), the stock has yet to be discovered by the wide market. As new information is revealed to the public and the interest increases, things move into the "awareness" phase. Increased awareness triggers a "mania" phase —the phase when new heights generate increased expectations. When expectations are positive, stock prices increase, and this attracts more investors (aka "dumb money"), pushing quotes higher and higher and disregarding the fundamentals. This is driven by greed, as people expect that the "buy high, sell higher" game they just entered will continue. On the other hand, when stock prices reach a level considered to be too high, the fear of losing it all drives the prices down (the "blow-off" phase). Fear is a much stronger emotion than greed; this explains why stock prices fall much faster in a downturn, and when they reach bottom, it is lower than the level where the upturn started.

THE CLASSIC BUBBLE WAVE

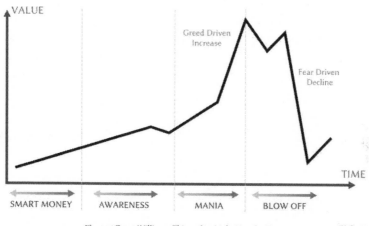

"Source: Grant Williams, Things that Make You Go Hmmm"   FIG. 8

As you have probably noticed, I said that "traditionally, stock prices have been calculated based on expectations." I used the word "traditionally" because that was valid in a time when all decisions about stock exchange transactions were made by humans. You can probably recall those images of stock exchange floors where highly agitated brokers are speaking into three phones in the same time, looking in ten directions, and waving their hands to communicate with each other in a sign language that only they understand. Nowadays, most of the trading decisions are made by computers. "Greed" and "fear" are no longer human emotional elements—they are instead components of sophisticated algorithms using key words in news feeds and advanced mathematics and analysis. Simply put, a computer program "reads and interprets" the news about a certain corporation, analyzes market information (trends, sales quotes, buy quotes, and volumes), and then makes a decision to sell or buy a certain stock. The increased shifting between up and down trends is no longer the result of human rational or emotional decisions, but of computer algorithms. In a matter of fraction of a second, a cascade of sell and buy orders can be placed in the market, pushing prices in one or another direction.

Second, trading on a stock exchange is about *speed*, which is extremely important in this entire game. Billions have been invested into this race where the values of the corporations listed on the stock exchange are decided by who has the best algorithm and fastest connections—a phenomenon known as "high-frequency trading," where transactions are carried out within microseconds or even shorter (just to clarify, there are one million microseconds in one second).

In *Flash Boys*, a book that plumbs the depths of this phenomenon and practice, author Michael Lewis writes,

> The US stock market was now a class system, rooted in speed, of haves and have-nots. The haves paid for nanoseconds; the have-nots had no idea that a nanosecond had value. The haves enjoyed a perfect view of the market; the have-nots *never saw the market at all* (p. 69).

We will not argue here and now whether this is morally right or wrong or whether things have gone too far in this direction. This is not the purpose of this book. But if you want to invest in individual publicly listed stocks, you need to understand that the stock market has different games, each with its own rules. You have to be aware of which games you need to stay away from, because you have no chance to compete. If you sit at home and trade online, you have to be aware that there is still a delay between the moment something happens on the exchange and the moment you click the button. Depending on your Internet connection and the wiring path to the servers of the exchanges, this delay may be short enough to give you the feeling of trading in real time. Most computer screens have a "refresh rate" of 100 images per second; as the image on your screen is updated 100 times every second, each image stays on the screen for 1/100 of a second, that is, 10,000 microseconds. As long as the "real time" transactions are carried out in a matter of microseconds, thousands of transactions have been already carried out on the exchange while you were waiting for your screen to update. You have absolutely no chance to *notice* them, let alone to *react* to them!

Another aspect of online trading is that we need to be aware of the *structure of the exchanges*. Many believe (as I did myself) that when we go online to buy and sell stocks, we somehow connect to one single computer that carries all the transaction. For instance, if we want to buy some Coca Cola stocks on the New York Stock Exchange (NYSE), we think that our order is somehow routed to the supercomputer located in the NYSE basement on Wall Street and is processed in real time together with millions of other orders. Or, if we want to buy or sell some Apple stocks on NASDAQ, we are directed to another supercomputer that carries out all transactions for companies listed on this exchange. This is very far from the truth. In fact, online trading of stocks is not carried out in a centralized manner, as many of us believe, but on dozens of supercomputers tied together in a high-speed network. Depending on the way they operate, these computers are called "exchanges" and "dark pools." They are owned by private companies, including stockbrokers, and the reason some of them are called "dark pools" is that there is no transparency regarding how the orders are processed on those computers.

That means that, when you open your online trading account with one particular stockbroker, there is a great chance for you to be connected to his *private exchange*. If you place an order to buy, let's say, ten Apple stocks, the exchange will first try to match your buy order with a corresponding sell order placed by another customer. If another of the broker's customers wants to sell ten Apple stocks, the system will sell you that customer's stocks without going out to the market. Only if there is no matching order on your broker's exchange will the system go out on the market and find the stocks you are looking for. Of course, there is a mechanism to update all the bids and offers for all US stocks (it's called SIP—Securities Information Processor—and this is the "official" information that you see on your monitor when you trade online), but in an environment where microseconds matter, there will always be differences. And it is exactly these differences that create a front-running opportunity for "high-frequency traders"—companies with superfast connections to different exchanges, allowing them to register your buy order and go out on the market (that is, on other exchanges) and find a matching sell order. They will simply buy the stocks you are looking for and sell them to you, making a small, but safe, profit.

In the same book, Flash Boys, Michael Lewis explains,

> In a paper published in February 2013, a team of researchers at the University of California, Berkeley, showed that the SIP [Securities Information Processor] price of Apple stock and the price seen by traders with faster channels of market information differed 55,000 times in a single day. That meant that there were 55,000 times a day when a HFT [high-frequency trader] could exploit the SIP generated ignorance of the wider market.

Does all this mean that you should never trade stocks online? Definitely not! But you have to be aware of what is going on, and your strategy should be based on *time frames where high speed and quick reaction is less relevant.*

Third, investing in public stocks is about the generally accepted *focus on short-term results*, the so-called *quarterly capitalism*. Investors expect stocks to constantly increase, and this requires increased profits from one quarter to another. As most CEOs are rewarded based on the performance of their company's stocks, they make decisions that increase profits in the short term, giving lower priority to the long-term goals. Investments in research and development, training, and employee benefits may be postponed in order to cut costs and provide "shareholder value."

According to a survey conducted by McKinsey & Company and Canada Pension Plan Investment Board (CPPIB) of more than 1,000 CEOs and board members,

> Seventy-nine percent of the respondents felt especially pressured to demonstrate strong financial performance over a period of just two years or less and [. . .] 44 percent said they use a time horizon of less than three years in setting strategy. The same study also pointed out that managers are fully aware of the drawbacks of short-term focus: [. . .] 86 percent declared that using a longer time horizon to make business decisions would positively affect corporate performance in a number of ways, including strengthening financial returns and increasing innovation (www.mckinsey.com/insights/leading_in_the_21st_century /focusing_capital_on_the_long_term).

IKEA, the Swedish furniture and home decoration retailer, is probably the best example of successful long-term growth without the pressure of the stock market. Many say that the founder, Ivar Kamprad, was able to make the right strategic decisions to ensure constant growth over decades just because he didn't have other investors to report to. Instead of struggling to meet profit expectations and keep analysts happy, Kamprad preferred to invest in the long sustainable growth—and the result speaks for itself.

Fourth, investment in public stocks is about *artificial increase of stock quotes due to buyback strategies*. I mentioned before that the price of a stock on the stock exchange is based on a multiplier of the profits (the so-called P/E factor). Let us go back to the example of a company that has 1,000,000 stocks, makes a profit of $1,000,000 per year, and the stock price is $10. The profit per share (called Earnings per Share, or EPS) is $1—that is, the total profit of $1,000,000 divided by 1,000,000 (the number of stocks in the company). The P/E is 10, because the price is $10 and the EPS is $1.

What happens if the management of the company decides to take a $5,000,000 loan from a bank and buys back 500,000 stocks? This buying back means that the stocks are bought on the market and then eliminated from the share capital of the company. In this case, the company still makes a $1,000,000 profit. But because the number of existing remaining stocks is only 500,000, the EPS is now $2 (the profit of $1,000,000 is divided by 500,000 stocks). If the stock price remains at $10, the P/E factor becomes 5. But the company's ability to generate profit is still there, and investors will consider this stock as "undervalued." Because they are willing to accept a P/E of 10 for this stock, they will buy stocks pushing the price toward $20, which is an EPS of $2 multiplied by a factor of 10.

The fact that company now has a loan of $5,000,000 is important, but this seems to be less relevant nowadays, when corporations have easy access to cheap financing due to very low interest rates. Unfortunately, this has become a very commonly used technique to inflate stock prices—companies take up loans to buy back their stocks. This means that, on their balance sheets, they keep their stock capital at the price of increasing liabilities. Even when corporations do not take up loans to buy back stocks, they use their own profits to do it. This is also a very bad long-term strategy because, instead of reinvesting those profits in research, developing new technologies and products, or simply expanding the business, something that would create and maintain competitive advantages, those profits are used to artificially boost the price of the stocks.

All the challenges listed above are not meant to discourage anybody from investing in stocks listed on the stock exchange, as the stock market has always been and always will be a good playground for investments. But in order to be successful in this game, you should definitely understand how it is played.

Having said all this about stocks of publicly held corporations, let us turn our attention toward *privately held* corporations. These are smaller companies that get capital through various alternative channels—members of the family or community, acquaintances, or investor networks. Investing in this kind of company presents a few advantages, the most important being that, most of the time, you have a direct connection to the company and the person who runs it. You invest in it because it's a business area that you know very well, or you simply trust the people. This gives you the possibility of closely following the development of the company and getting information firsthand, without having to wait months to get official quarterly reports, as you do when owning public stocks.

On the other hand, while you may have close contact with the management, you may not have much to say about how the business should be run. Generally, these companies have an entrepreneurial culture, meaning that one or a few managers control everything with a strong hand, and they are not always open to other people's ideas. This may also mean that the entire business becomes very vulnerable if, for some reason, key people leave the floor.

If the investment is made in the early stages of a growth company, the potential for return is really huge, exceeding many times the return offered by publicly owned stocks. But this is valid only for the right companies that offer the right type of products or services with the right timing. According to data published by venture capital institutions and associations, the success rate of start-up businesses is somewhere between 25 and 35 percent. This means that, for every success story we read about, there are two or three failures we never hear about. If the venture capital industry has been growing so much in recent decades, it is because the returns on successful investments were high enough to not only offset but also exceed the losses registered with failed businesses.

But undoubtedly, the main challenge of owning stocks in privately held corporations is the *lack of liquidity*. The closer ties you have with the company, the harder it will be to sell your shares. You may be excited to own a 25 percent stake in your cousin's restaurant, but you should not expect to meet with the same type of excitement if you go out of your family's circle. If you for some reason decide to sell your shares, you have to be prepared to wait a long time until you find a buyer willing to pay an acceptable price.

In addition to the challenge of selling your shares, the second difficulty is getting the right price. The pricing of publicly listed stocks may have its peculiarities, as I described earlier, but still those prices reflect a general perception about a company's prospects, a perception that is created and shared by *many* investors. In the case of a privately held company, there is no benchmark of public opinion, and consequently, it is hard to define a price upon which both seller and buyer can agree. The final outcome is a matter of who has the most interest in making the deal, and if the seller is the one who has this interest, he will have to accept the buyer's conditions.

Finally, there is always the question of whether stocks (equities) are *tangible* assets or *paper* assets. The answer is that they can be both—depending on which stock we are talking about. I mentioned before that a stock is a share of a company's assets. The assets of some companies are clearly tangible, such as goods, infrastructure, or commodities. For instance, oil companies have rights to extract oil from the ground, mining companies extract metals, railway companies own railways and transportation carts, and real estate companies own buildings. Owning stocks of these companies is the same as owning a share of their assets. In other words, the stock is a paper asset, but there are real, tangible goods behind it.

On the other hand, some companies have assets that are not tangible, but they are valued because they provide something of interest to a wide audience. A mass media corporation is valued based on how much attention it gets from TV viewers or radio listeners. A social media company is valuable only as long it has users. When all this interest disappears, there is nothing left—of the company or its value. Of course, there are always some tangible assets in these companies—TV stations have cameras and broadcast equipment, Internet companies have computers and servers, but the value of these assets is much lower than the value given to a high user count or audience. In addition, these tangible assets are the kind of assets that quickly depreciate.

Blockbuster is a company that started small and grew significantly during the '80s and '90s, taking advantage of the technological developments in the home entertainment sector. As one of the biggest video rental stores, the company was purchased in 1994 by Viacom for $8.4 billion—a value based mainly on the company's ability to meet the need for an inexpensive home entertainment experience. Booming throughout the VHS and early DVD eras, Blockbuster ignored the technological developments that came later on, when companies like Redbox started to aggressively set up DVD kiosks, and Netflix steadily took advantage of better streaming technology. Ironically, in 2000, Blockbuster turned down the chance to acquire Netflix for $50 million (*www.fastcompany.com/1690654/blockbuster-bankruptcy-decade-decline*). In the end, the company filed for bankruptcy in 2010, and all stores were closed during the ensuing years. Although most of the stores were sold based on their "brick and mortar" value, this value was way below what the company was once worth.

In conclusion, when deciding to invest in stocks, one should carefully analyze the underlying values and assets, being aware that any value based on technological lead is extremely volatile because new technologies are continuously being developed. The same is also valid for value-based public perception and interest, due to human nature that always looks for something new.

Bonds

Bonds are also a very common category of investments and are considered to be the necessary balance to stocks. A bond represents nothing more than an "I Owe You" (IOU) certificate, meaning that if you invest in those bonds, you become a creditor to the institution that issued the bonds. When in need of funding, a certain institution will go to the market and issue bonds to collect the funds it needs. Bonds can be issued by private corporations or public institutions like governments or municipalities. All bonds have a maturity date, which may be shorter or longer, depending on the type of the bond and the need for financing of the institution, and they pay an interest rate, which is the return you are getting as investor.

Let's say that a company needs $10,000,000 to finance a project and chooses to issue 5-year bonds with a face value of $1,000 at an interest rate of 6 percent per year. The total amount of $10,000,000 is divided into 10,000 bonds with a *face value* of $1,000 each. When you, as investor, buy one bond, you pay $1,000 and collect $60 every year (which is the 6 percent interest rate applied to the face value of $1,000). After five years (on the maturity day), you get your $1,000 back. In other words, throughout the entire lifetime of this bond, you get your initial money back plus $300 that you collected during the five years. Bonds issued by municipalities and governments work in the same way.

Bonds balance stocks in the following way: while stocks may provide higher returns due to price appreciation, they are also riskier. On the other hand, bonds provide a lower return, but it is fixed and safer. In other words, when you invest in stocks, you may get a higher return, but there is a chance you may not get it at all. When you invest in bonds, you may not get much, but at least you know what you are getting, and there is a good chance you won't lose anything. This is why, when structuring investments in stocks and bonds, a portfolio that contains 60 percent stocks and 40 percent bonds has been traditionally considered to offer the right "balance" between return and risk. If the share of the stocks exceeds 60 percent, the portfolio is considered "aggressive," while if the stock portion is less than 60 percent, the portfolio is considered "conservative."

The safety aspect of the bonds has been conferred by the fact that, in case of bankruptcy, bond holders are creditors to the institution, and therefore, when a corporation is liquidated, creditors are paid before stockholders. Until a few years ago, municipalities and governments were considered by conventional wisdom to be "safe havens." The last years have proven that this is far from the truth. The sovereign bond crisis in Europe and the famous City of Detroit bankruptcy in the US showed that not even bond holders are always guaranteed their money back. All these bonds are guaranteed by the full faith of the issuer, be it a municipality or a government. But as we all know, with few exceptions, all these institutions operate with huge deficits—meaning that, year after year, their expenses are higher than the revenues they generate. The difference is covered by new bonds, and this is why the public debt continues to increase year after year. Older debt is never paid back from existing revenues; this is done only by issuing new debt, adding new deficits to older debt—a phenomenon called "kicking the can down the road." This practice has been used for decades and is an important part of the financial global system, where all money originates as debt and requires more and more debt in order to continue (something I discussed in Chapter 4 concerning the true nature of money). In the end, all this is just a game of numbers. This system will continue as long as there are investors willing to join the game, and when that is over, as long as new financial instruments will be created that sustain the entire financial system.

Like stocks, bonds are also sold on exchanges—meaning that somebody who has invested in a bond can sell it to someone else before the maturity date. Let's go back to the example above, where we assume you bought a 5-year bond with a face value of $1,000 that pays 6 percent per year interest. Remember, I said that this bond pays you $60 every year, and at maturity, after five years, will pay you back the face value of $1,000. But what if you want to recover your money after you keep the bond for, let's say, two years? You can sell it on the market, and the price at the time you want to sell is defined by several factors, including the remaining time until maturity and the evolution of the general interest rate. As a basic rule, you should remember that *bond prices and interest rates move in opposite directions*. Why is that?

- *When interest rates decline, bond prices increase*. This is because, if new bonds are issued at, let's say, 4 percent interest, other investors will prefer to buy your bond offering 6 percent interest rather than putting their money into a bond paying only 4 percent. This means that they are willing to pay more than the $1,000 face value now, in order to get the 6 percent return.

- *When interest rates increase, bond prices drop*. This is because, if new bonds are issued at, say, 8 percent, investors will prefer to put their money into those new bonds. On the other hand, a buyer may be willing to accept a 6 percent return instead of 8 percent if he can get your bond for less than the $1,000 face value. In other words, he gets less every year until maturity, but will get back the $1,000 face value at maturity, which is more than what he paid when he bought the bond from you.

Mutual Funds

Presented by many as the ideal investment vehicle, mutual funds operate following a simple principle: they collect money from different investors into a "pool" and then allocate that amount into different assets, such as stocks, bonds, real estate, or commodities. Buying a share of a mutual fund, which is equivalent to investing in the mutual fund, means that you have a slice of a wider portfolio of assets. Every mutual fund is administered by a fund manager, who makes all decisions with regard to allocation of the pool of money—normally within the limitations given by its mandate. Mutual funds can have a wide allocation (mix of stocks and bonds, possibly following certain stock exchange indexes), or they can be very narrow and specific, investing in only one industry. Definitely, there are several advantages for an individual investor in using mutual funds.

The most important is that they are considered less risky, because fund managers do all the homework of studying the companies and types of assets to invest in. It is presumed that the manager has access to resources that individual investors do not have and they make better choices on when to buy or sell individual stocks or assets. Also, because they spread the pool of money into many assets, mutual funds provide the diversification that less-experienced investors absolutely need.

Shares of mutual funds are also easy to sell and buy because they are traded on exchanges like any other stock and can be traded with the help of any stockbroker, even online. The price of the shares in mutual funds is based on their NAV (Net Asset Value) and represents the value of all assets in which the fund is invested. As the value of these assets increases and decreases continuously, the NAV is also continuously updated.

Another important feature is the possibility of reinvesting the return. A mutual fund can have return on investments in the form of stock dividends, interest paid by bond issuers, or capital gains from trading assets, and you, as the fund's shareholder, receive a part of this return. In most cases, this return can be plowed back into the fund—something that is very important in a long-term investment strategy. But there are also challenges associated with investing in mutual funds.

Costs are one important aspect. All of the fund's operating costs and management fees have to be paid out of the returns on the fund's investments. Normally, fund managers are paid as a percentage of managed assets with a guaranteed minimum amount. If the fund performs well, there is enough gain to cover both the costs and give a return to investors. But if the fund performs poorly, the management fees and the other costs have to be paid anyway, creating a double loss—not only the lost value of fund's assets but also the second cut, which is the fees.

It is important to realize that mutual fund shares are paper assets, and hence are extremely volatile. The more volatile the assets the fund invests in, the more volatile is the fund. When the value of the assets decreases, so does the value of the fund. Therefore, the diversification mentioned in previous sections has to be understood correctly: mutual funds provide diversification within the same asset class (paper assets like stocks and bonds) and not across different asset classes. In other words, a mutual fund protects the investor from loss caused by individual stocks but does not protect from losses if the entire market drops.

As with any other paper asset, the moral hazard is also a very important challenge to take into consideration. In times when the interest rates are low and access to cheap financing is available, fund managers who take speculative risks are the rule rather than the exception. Covered by credit ratings and well-formulated disclaimers, they engage in speculative operations focusing on quick gains, and do so without any remorse, because "everybody else is doing it anyway."

Finally, limitations in the fund's manager mandate may also be a challenge. Many funds' statutes require managers to be almost 100 percent invested in stocks and bonds—meaning they are not allowed to keep a part of the funds in cash, except for a small portion used to cover current expenses. If the fund's manager expects a decline in stock or bond prices, it makes sense for him to sell and keep some cash on hand while waiting for the downturn in order to buy at lower prices. This would be the right decision, but if the mandate requires 100 percent investment, he has to buy and keep financial assets that he personally thinks are overvalued.

Real Estate

Real estate is one of the investment areas where great fortunes have been built—and lost. As with other types of investments, due to the specific focus of this book, I will just highlight a few facts about investing in real estate. These are things I have learned and noticed either through my own experience or as they have been presented to me by acquaintances and friends who invest in real estate.

The first thing I would like to address is the misconception that "your home is an investment." This is indeed a very controversial standpoint, because we all have been taught that our home is a part of our wealth, and this is why our home is a good investment.

When defining assets and investments, an investment was defined as "release of resources that generates a future flow of income." But buying our own home does not produce any income—a point made clear by Robert Kiyosaki in his book Rich Dad, Poor Dad. When buying a home financed 80 percent with a 30-year mortgage, we end up paying over the double the price we initially paid. If we take into account all taxes, repairs, and home improvement costs (aka "pride of ownership"), we find out that we have paid out at least three times the initial price of the house. That shouldn't sound like a good investment to anybody! But let's think for a second about who tells us that our home is a good investment . . . it's real estate agents and banks, and both make good money every time a transaction is concluded. Does this mean that you should rent rather than buying the house you want to live in? Definitely not. But there are two things to do.

First, understand that the primary purpose of your home is to provide you and your family shelter. It is about making it nice, homey, and cozy—in other words, the nest where you and your loved ones can have a great family experience. You add things and improvements because they provide a better quality of life, not because some day you are going to sell the home for a profit.

Second, you need to take into account all costs before you buy. Studies show that if you come to a place with the knowledge that you are going to be in it fewer than five years, renting may be cheaper than buying a house and selling it later. Renting is indeed money going right out of your pocket, but so are commissions to realtors (two times, both when you buy and when you sell), property taxes, and repairs. And, during the first years, your mortgage payment covers mostly the interest anyway—which is also pure loss (although tax deductible, still a loss). All these add up to a significant amount. Assuming that you sell the property for the same amount you paid for it, the five-year horizon represents the breakeven of all these costs.

Now, if you agree that your home is not an investment, how do you need to look at it?

- If you are in the place where you expect to be for the longer run, find a house that meets your present and future estimated realistic needs.

- Do not fall into the trap of buying something bigger than you need just because somebody (typically your real estate agent) is telling you that it's going to appreciate in value and the housing market is on the rise again.

- Do not go for the maximum amount that the bank is willing to qualify you for. Dave Ramsey, author of *Total Money Makeover*, recommends that your monthly payment should not exceed 25 percent of your take-home pay, and you should always choose a 15-year mortgage.

- All costs that you have to cover to keep the property in good shape, and the interest, are *expenses* that you willingly pay in order to provide a *home* for your family.

- If there will be any appreciation of the property, let it be an additional gain *without making it a part of your initial decision process*. If appreciation comes, it's good for you, but if it doesn't come, it's not a tragedy. You lived happily with your family for fifteen years in a house that now is paid for.

Now, since we have clarified that real estate investing is not about buying your own home, let us review some facts related to investing in residential real estate. We will focus on residential because the other types of real estate (commercial, office buildings and industrial, shopping centers) are too specialized and require knowledge and funding beyond the possibilities of a starting investor.

Real estate is the best example of leveraged investment. We will describe in a later section the significant difference between debt and leverage. But for now, in order to illustrate this, let's assume that you have $100,000 to invest.

One option would be to buy a single-family home for $100,000 and rent it out for, let's say, $10,000 per year. The cash flow after paying your taxes, repairs, and all other maintenance costs, probably somewhere in the range $5,000 to $6,000, represents your return on the investment.

The second option would be to buy a multifamily apartment building (let's say six units), where your $100,000 represents a 25 percent down payment for a $400,000 property. The balance of $300,000 can be financed with a mortgage. In this case, your revenues are much higher because you collect rent from several units. Although the individual rent may be lower than for an apartment than a single-family home, the total amount collected is significantly higher (probably somewhere around $50–55,000 per year). Out of this amount, around $25,000 has to go to service the debt. And after paying taxes and all other repairs and operational expenses, you are left with an yearly cash-flow of approximately $12,000 to $15,000.

Although the numbers above are only illustrative, the point is that the same initial investment can lead to much higher returns. But this is not the only thing that makes real estate a good leveraged investment. In fact, there is another aspect that is more important—and it is related to the equity built over time. In the first option, the owner's equity is $100,000 to start with, and assuming that property price does not change, this equity remains the same over years. In the second option, the owner's equity is the same to start with ($100,000), but it constantly increases over years. Every monthly mortgage payment covers both interest and principal—meaning that for every month that goes by, the owner's equity builds until the loan is fully paid and the owner fully owns a $400,000 property. And most important is the fact that this equity buildup did not come out of the owner's own pocket, but out of the rent paid by tenants. In other words, tenants paid for the owner's equity.

Before moving on, let us clarify one important difference between the two. The first option (buying a $100,000 single home and renting it out) is *an investment in a 100% owned tangible asset.* All rent income goes directly into the owner's pocket. It may be more or less depending on the economic conditions, or if markets are more or less favorable for renting, but, nonetheless, the owner keeps the revenue. Even if he has to lower the rent in order to avoid vacancy, the asset still produces a return. It may not be the ideal return, but the money still comes month after month. In the second option (buying a multi-unit apartment building, where the $100,000 represents a down payment), the investor is tied to a mortgage, which is *a financial product,* and he is obligated to making monthly payments to the lender. If, for some reason, the rent income does not cover the minimum payment, the investor must cover the difference from other sources, otherwise, he risks defaulting on the loan and losing the property.

But there are also other limitations that need to be well understood.

One of them is that 0 percent down means 100 percent financed property purchase. This "nothing down" topic has received a lot of attention within the real estate investing community. Simply, it means that a buyer finds a motivated seller who is willing to also be the financing party. Nothing is paid at the time of transaction, but the buyer commits to pay monthly to the seller an amount that covers some principal and some interest that is acceptable to the seller.

It seems like a great model, doesn't it? What could be better for a buyer—especially if this is an investment property? You buy it, you rent it out, collect the rent, pay the seller the agreed amount, and pocket the balance—which may be a few hundred dollars every month. Entire books, articles, and videos on the Internet are dedicated to this topic, taking the most extreme positions—from the most favorable ("that's the only way to do it") to the most critical ("don't even think about that"). On the question of whether this is a good model, my answer is both *yes* and *no*. Everything depends on the seller, the buyer, and the property in question. Based on my own experience as landlord, I will make a few comments about it.

One thing to understand is that people who recommend this model have done it for years, and they continue because they have become experts with this model. Their advice is valuable, but if you decide to go down this route, you have to be prepared to make some costly mistakes or fall into some traps yourself—simply because each circumstance (in this case the seller and property) is unique.

Not all properties are good properties. This is why is important to carefully examine all elements: the seller, his motivation to sell, and the property. Some people sell because of personal reasons—family situation, sickness, moving, retirement—and these may well be valid motivations. But some sell because the property is distressed to a point that they don't want to deal with it anymore and they are willing to accept any conditions just to get rid of it. In this case, the questions are: What is wrong with the property, and what does it take to make it a positive cash flow investment? Some properties are in such bad shape that it may take months or even years to turn them around—you may need to make additional investments to make it code compliant or deal with bad tenants whom you may need to evict. All these consume both money and time.

You also need to take into consideration that while the idea of pocketing a few hundreds of dollars every month seems good on paper, this money completely disappears in case you have a vacancy or you have to deal with a major repair. Even if you are a handy person and can fix many things yourself, many cities regard rental properties as *commercial activity*, and therefore, some types of work, such as electrical, plumbing, or HVAC, require permits and execution by licensed contractors. There is a huge difference between being a *homeowner* and a *landlord*. A simple visit from a plumber or electrician may cost you a couple hundred dollars, not including any parts they install or replace. This is enough to eat up all your cash flow for one month. If you have a one-month vacancy and collect no rent, this is also equivalent to several months of your cash flow. All this means that the 0 percent down model may work for you well if the following conditions are met:

- it is the right property—meaning it's code compliant and there are no technical issues attached to it;

- it has the right location—meaning it is not located in a downtrending area where it may be difficult to keep quality tenants;

- you have a cash reserve that allows you to make payments to the seller even if there is a vacancy;

- you have enough reserves to cover repairs when there is need for them.

Real estate investments allow you to deduct all related expenses. In addition to leverage, there is another major advantage of investing in real estate. If you own properties that are leased out, you will be able to deduct from your income all expenses related to property taxes, insurance, management fees (if the property is managed by a separate company), advertising costs, legal and accounting fees, preventive maintenance and repairs, utilities (if the lease agreement specifies that you are the one covering these), yard work, and snow removal. Trips to and from the property are also deductible, provided that you can document that inspecting the property was the main reason for your trip.

Depreciation is also another important incentive that makes real estate attractive as investment. Depreciation is considered a "loss of the value" of the property and is accounted for as an expense, reducing the owner's taxable income while, in reality, the amount booked as depreciation never leaves the owner's pocket (or bank account). The whole topic is much more complicated than that, and rules are different from one jurisdiction to another. This is why I will not go further into details in this book. But the principle to be kept in mind is that you as a landlord can write off a part of the value of your property without affecting your cash flow.

In addition to investing directly in investment properties, it is also possible to invest indirectly, by purchasing shares in real estate companies or REITs (Real Estate Investment Trusts). While these may spare the investor the hassle of dealing with tenants and fixing toilets, they are still stocks of companies and therefore, more risky.

Investing in Precious Metals

Precious metals represent a very special area of investments. For all other assets, be they stocks, bonds, or real estate, there is a general common understanding about the particularities of each category. When it comes to precious metals, there are very different camps with very different opinions. We have all heard the old saying, "not all that glitters is gold." A modern translation in today's world would be, "not everything we call gold, is gold." When talking about precious metals, I have in mind four different categories: gold, silver, platinum, and palladium. During recent years, rhodium, due to its increasing use in inexpensive jewelry, also became considered a precious metal. All these are rare, meaning they aren't as common as other metals, and consequently, the costs to extract and refine them are much higher. They have special qualities that make them good in very special uses, where other metals cannot be used. These two particularities, being rare and being used for special purposes, create the dual character of precious metals.

On one hand, precious metals are associated with being a *store of value over time and borders*. Throughout history, borders have been moved back and forth, empires have grown and collapsed, money (in the form of currencies) has been created and disappeared; still, precious metals have been recognized as safe havens by everybody and made possible the transfer of wealth from one system to another. As *stores of value*, precious metals are hoarded by people who lack confidence in paper currencies or in the authorities' ability to create wealth.

On the other hand, special industrial uses make these metals traded also as *commodities*, where price is determined by the available stock above ground and ratio between future supply and demand. Although all the metals mentioned (gold, silver, platinum, palladium, and rhodium) present this dual character, their role is different depending on how much is hoarded and how much is used by industry. This can be summarized as follows.

Gold is, by far, the most used metal for store of value. It is used in *bullion* (bars and coins) and jewelry. Gold has some industrial uses, as a commodity, but this share is so tiny compared to the total quantity of gold that we can easily ignore it. Although some may argue that jewelry or dental uses make gold a commodity, this is wrong, because gold is not consumed in the process. A commodity is something that is used and consumed in order to satisfy a need, and most commodities, after consumption, cannot be recovered in their original form. All gold used for jewelry and dental purposes can be easily recovered and, if required, refined to a higher degree of purity. In conclusion, *gold is the store of value par excellence.*

Silver has both uses, and the relation between its use as store of value and as commodity has changed a few times throughout history. Silver is indispensable in many high-technology areas (cell phones, computers, solar panels, water purification), and the growth of these sectors in recent decades has shifted the balance more in the direction of silver being a commodity. At the same time, people who were interested in storing precious metals preferred to buy gold, which is much more compact. Simply, it takes much more space to store the same value of silver as it does for gold.

For centuries, gold and silver were used as money, and although paper money was issued, those papers represented nothing but redeemable certificates of a certain quantity of gold and silver. This is the core of the *gold standard*—where any person holding a banknote could go to the issuer and get the equivalent quantity of gold or silver.

Platinum and palladium also have the same dual character, but I will not focus on these metals for now. I will concentrate on gold and silver, as these have received the most attention from the general public, investors, analysts, and commentators. There are very many opinions about precious metals, and the opportunity to invest in precious metal is one of the most controversial topics in economics and finance. This is why I will try below to make some common-sense comments.

Rarity alone does not determine classification as precious metal. Many other metals are much more rare than gold, silver, platinum, palladium, and rhodium. They are hard to find, the process of extraction is complicated, and they have very specific industrial uses; therefore, the prices per ounce may be even higher than the metals mentioned. Still, they are not considered precious because these metals have no general acceptance as stores of value. Those metals will remain commodities—as just some expensive and absolutely necessary ingredients in certain industries.

A clear distinction exists between physical metal and paper metal. The idea of "paper gold" or "paper silver" may sound like a paradox. And it indeed is, because this is probably the number one source of confusion when it comes to investing in precious metals. Simply put, there are two different markets out there.

The physical market. This is where the object of trade is bullion (bars and coins) of precious metal. Somebody who wants to buy a precious metal will find a dealer—a store or online—and get a physical delivery of the purchased metal. Further, the buyer can decide if he wants to get the metal in his hands (i.e., buy some coins at the store and take them home) or have it shipped to, and stored in, a vault. Having the bars or coins stored at home has the clear advantage of directly possessing the valuable assets, but the drawback of theft and burglary risk. Storing in a vault is an option, especially for larger quantities. Some companies specialize in this type of service, providing insured secure vaults where an owner's metals are stored in a protected manner. In addition to the psychological factor ("someone else is keeping my gold"), the drawback is that this service is not free of charge.

The paper market. This is the market where the object of trade is represented by *paper certificates* or *contracts that are related to precious metals.* In other words, this is a market where different *financial instruments* are traded, not the physical metal itself. One important aspect of this paper market, maybe the most important, is that sellers and buyers have no interest in possessing the metal; they deal with paper assets at hand, focusing on making profits from the trade.

Without going into details, I can say that such financial instruments can take several forms, and the variety and complexity of this market forms the foundation of what many experts call "precious metals manipulation." We can consider *leasing arrangements* (where a certain quantity of gold is borrowed from a central bank and used to back shares in ETFs—Exchange Traded Funds), or *future contracts* (where the future production of gold mines is already sold in advance). And of course, there are other kinds of derivative instruments based on such arrangements.

It is up to each individual involved in dealing with precious metal to take a position whether this is manipulation or rigging—or not. We just observe that all these artificial arrangements seem to be nothing more than a part of the entire financial system—to create inventive financial instruments that allow participants to charge different kind of fees and make short-term paper profits.

Regardless of how one views the entire precious metal play, there is one indubitable fact—the total amount of metals traded as paper metal is many times greater than the underlying quantity of physical metal. In an interview with independent journalist Lars Schall, Grant Williams, portfolio and strategy adviser to Vulpes Investment Management in Singapore, author of the financial newsletter *Things That Make You Go Hmmm . . .* (ttmygh.com) and founder of *Real Vision TV* (realvisiontv.com), pointed out that for each ounce of physical gold that backs precious metal exchanges, around 100 ounces of paper gold are in transaction. In other words, approximately 100 certificates, each denominated as 1 ounce, are issued based on one single ounce of existing gold. Why is this possible? Because the general expectation in the financial industry is that no more that 1 percent of certificate holders will ask for the physical metal itself.

Grant Williams clarifies the difference between "price of gold," which is *the price of one ounce of physical metal,* and "gold price," which is *the price of a piece of paper saying 'one ounce of gold.'* (In fact, it's not even a piece of paper, just a digital certificate containing this wording, but for argument's sake we will call it "paper"). This is also why there are certain obstacles when trying to move from paper to physical. When someone says, "I invest in gold" and then buys a 1-ounce share in an ETF gold fund, this is not the same as having one ounce of physical gold that can be claimed any time. Those shares represent *unallocated* gold, meaning that nowhere in the world is there a piece of metal registered as owned by that particular investor.

Redeeming the physical metal by an ETF share owner is not easy. Some ETFs do not even allow it—when the investor sells his shares, he gets cash. In this case, if the *spot price* has increased, it may even be a good investment. The investor paid some cash and gets back more cash—with no interference in the physical metal ground. Some ETFs allow conversion of the shares into physical metal if minimum quantity requirements are met. Normally, these requirements are beyond the reach of the individual small investor. It is important to understand that the spot price of precious metals, as it is daily listed and made reference to in all analytic commentaries in the media, is not determined, as one might expect in the physical market, by supply and demand, but in the paper market, where the traded volumes are much larger than existing metals.

This is why, when buying physical metal, any buyer has to pay a premium—a fee to be paid over the spot price. When the physical demand increases, the premium gets higher. If the physical demand increases too much, it may not even be possible to buy metals. As long as the available quantity of physical metal is much smaller than the paper metal that determines the spot price, even a small move in physical demand will have a stronger impact on the premiums or even availability.

Another consequence is that, if the perception as a safe haven gets more public support, this effect is multiplied because the general supply will decrease significantly. Wealthy individuals who hold physical precious metals do not have to sell them to make ends meet anyway, and anyone willing to sell will do his best to wait for further increases of price.

Now, before moving on, we can raise a common-sense question related to "price of gold" and "gold price." Having in mind that there are approximately 100 pieces of paper *all claiming the same ounce of gold*, and investors are willing to pay over $1,200 for each of those papers, what is the real "price of gold"?

Investing in physical precious metals does not produce returns. There are people stating, "Gold is not a good investment because a brick of gold in your cabinet will produce nothing." Personally, I would use this statement to support the argument that "gold is money," because a stack of cash in your cabinet, even if it's the size of a brick, will not produce anything either! In order to generate a return, money has to be invested. Keeping it in a cabinet is not investment. But the fact is that *possessing physical precious metals is not for the purpose of producing returns, but rather as a hedge against loss of value and purchasing power by paper currencies.* So the main reason for buying physical precious metals is not return, but protection.

For someone who does not believe in the long-term sustainability of paper currencies, buying precious metals makes a lot of sense. This kind of person will simply buy metals on a regular basis and pay the applicable price at the moment of purchase and will not be concerned about the evolution of prices. This person's mindset says, "I gave away some paper and I got in return something real." In fact, this kind of person will use any drop in the spot price as an opportunity to get more metals for the same amount of paper money. Also, they do not see paper money as a reference for value. For them, 1 ounce of gold or silver is the baseline; that value doesn't change. How much that is expressed in dollars, euros, or any other currency doesn't really matter—it's just a number expressed in a unit of measure that keeps changing. It is like a person traveling from the United States to Europe carrying a 50-pound suitcase. In Europe, the scale will show approximately 23 kilos. The suitcase is the same and the weight is the same; going from 50 down to 23 does not mean that he lost half of the luggage. The reverse is also true. Traveling from Europe to the US and going from 23 to 50 does not mean a doubling of the suitcase. It's just a different number because the measuring unit changes.

Most people, especially in countries that never experienced high inflation, are conditioned to think of paper money as a reference of value, as something that does not change. This is mainly because the change is slow. For somebody who takes paper money as a reference, buying precious metals in physical form does not make sense. On one hand, as I just pointed out, these metals do not produce any form of cash flow. On the other hand, the only form in which they may produce returns is by value appreciation—meaning that the prices (numbers) have to increase. This person's mindset is the following: "I buy now at this price and will be able to sell later at a higher price." Being vulnerable to high fluctuations and concerned over not losing the invested amount of paper money, this person will follow the spot price and be very happy if it goes up and very frustrated if it drops. This is why, for a person who has confidence in paper money as a measurement of value, buying physical metals does not seem to be a good idea.

* * *

A Few Final Considerations about Investments
As we have seen, there are no generally applicable "right" or "wrong" investment strategies. Each of them has its own advantages, risks, and challenges. Therefore, it is up to each individual to decide which assets are most suitable for one's own circumstances. Regardless of the choice, I have personally learned the hard way that there are a few important rules to be followed.

- Have a very good understanding of the playing field you want to invest in.

There is such an overwhelming abundance of materials that can help you understand the area of investment—and I would mention especially books and the Internet. I personally give less importance to articles and news because I consider these to be biased and manipulative, promoting different agendas. This can be said as well about books and the Internet, but these media have a lower threshold for entrance, and therefore, there is a much wider range of opinions and advice. While it's also true that any novice can spit out nonsense in front of a web camera (and many do!), there is also much valuable advice given by people who've "been there, done that." These people are normally not invited to radio and TV interviews and talk shows, as their opinions vary strongly from what editorial boards consider acceptable to be aired.

The more time you spend listening to and reading different opinions, the better equipped you will be to make good decisions. My experience also tells me that it's better to wait while gaining understanding, rather than jumping into unknown areas. This is hard, because sometimes there's a pressure to start doing something, and there is a feeling of losing opportunities. As I will point out in Chapter 9, where I discuss opportunities, there is always a difference between preparation and procrastination.

- Move ahead and learn as you go, but don't start running right away.

There is a moment when you've done enough study, and more knowledge can be gained only by experience. Waiting more means to procrastinate. But it's important to start on a small scale and operate at a lower level until you know the drill. As your confidence level increases, you can move to the next level.

- Limit your investments to what you can lose.

Especially when investing in paper assets and financial instruments, it's only a game of numbers—and many times it's pure gambling. Therefore, you should make sure that you don't gamble more than you can lose.

Jim Rogers, legendary investor, businessman, and author, explains in his book *Street Smarts*,

> Do not worry about making mistakes in life. It is good to lose money, to go broke at least once, and preferably twice. But if you are going to do it, do it early in your career. It is

better to go bust when you are talking about $20,000 than when you are talking about $20 million. Do it early and it is not the end of the world. Losing everything can be beneficial experience, because it teaches you how much you do not know. And if you can come back from a failure or two, chances are you are going to be more successful in the long run. [...] There is nothing wrong with failing if you learn from your mistakes.

Debt and Leverage

Debt and leverage is also an area where people express very different and controversial opinions, ranging from the most favorable, e.g., "everybody has debt" and "you can't build anything without debt," to the most unfavorable, e.g., "debt is evil." As with any other area of finances, things are not necessarily black and white, but much more nuanced. As I will point out in this section, debt is nothing but a tool, and like any other tool, it can help you tremendously when used correctly for the job that the tool was designed for and can harm you greatly when it's misused.

The purpose of debt is to use it as a lever in connection with your investment. This means that, when you make a certain investment decision, you borrow money so you can increase your purchase of an income-producing asset. As I will explain below, this is not about you buying a nicer car, new kitchen cabinets, a new plasma TV, or some of the latest designer fashions.

Understanding the Difference between Debt and Leverage

First of all, we need to address the issue of consumer debt—which represents indeed the bad alternative of debt, and, to make the point clear from the beginning, you should have none of it! Wealthy people understand the costs associated with buying things with money they do not have. They understand the concept of "living within their means," which is a good principle, but yet, they also work hard to expand their means. Regardless of what you buy, its value or payback time, the interest will make you pay at least double for that particular item or good. High-value assets can be financed at lower interest, but have a long payback time. Goods with lower value can be purchased using different arrangements of consumer credit with significantly higher interest rates.

"Small monthly payments," seemingly attractive to everybody, is one of the most powerful known marketing traps—no one will ever publicize that only a tiny fraction of that monthly payment represents principal, with the balance being interest and other charges. After all, paying double for the same thing just because we can have it now and pay later is nothing more than paying an equivalent amount for lack of patience as for the goods themselves. This is another example of why wealthy people develop patience, allowing them to always look for the best deals and pay down.

Interest is the price of "money now"—a reward for patience and a penalty for lack of patience. Seen from a saver's perspective, interest is the reward to the person who decides to postpone consumption and save. Flipping the coin, interest is the penalty paid by the person who doesn't have the patience to wait. This is why, when interest rates are fixed by central banks, a distortion is induced in the entire economy, especially when the rates are kept artificially low. The savers are punished because they are deprived of their reward for patience, and the debtors are rewarded. Unfortunately, it is obvious that it's not the individual borrowers who are rewarded, because they have to pay high interest for their consumer debt, but the financial sector—who can borrow cheaply from central banks and lend out to individuals at much higher rates.

Living in a comfortable home with a cozy environment is a natural desire for all human beings. Still, you have to recognize and accept that all furniture and decorations you buy to impress your cousins or neighbors are not real "assets." You may define a value for them when you buy your insurance, but you should be aware that there is a significant drop in value, called *depreciation*, when these items are moved from the store into your home. The same couch that you pay $2,000 for in store is probably not worth more than half of that when positioned in your living room just a few hours later. Why is that? The reason is that it is no longer a new couch, but a used one. If, in addition to that, you purchase it with a credit card that charges 12 to 15 percent interest per year and the entire amount is paid in 24 months, you end up paying at least $500 in interest. This is probably way more than what the couch is worth after two years.

On the other hand, wealthy people understand the difference between *personal debt* and *leverage*. This is why they avoid any form of "bad debt"—when it's acquired to purchase goods for personal consumption that depreciate in value. While some say, "any debt is bad debt," it is still an open debate whether leverage is good or as bad as any other debt. This is why it is important to understand the difference.

Consumer debt is nothing more than *consumption taken today and paid for later*. This may seem like a good deal. After all, what can be better than getting something now and paying later? Isn't it better than getting it now and paying for it now? Or isn't it better than getting it later and paying it later? If you wholeheartedly answer "yes" to these two questions, you have already fallen into the trap—a deceit that the banking system would like you to believe. To your comfort, this is a trap that most people fall into, and, just to be fair, I used to strongly believe it myself some years ago when I was in deep debt and I bragged about having a high credit limit! Indeed, the notion of getting it now and paying later may seem like a good deal, but it ignores the fact that debt represents a *claim on your future income*. And this has two major negative consequences for you.

First, it *strongly limits your future choices*. Most people make their *money* by trading in their *time* for it. Regardless of whether they are employees, self-employed professionals, or business owners, these people have to dedicate time in order to generate income. Because a significant part of this income is already claimed by the debt incurred earlier, the logical conclusion is that *debt makes a claim on your future time*. In other words, *being in debt is a form of modern serfdom—because it makes you the serf of your lender*. You may feel free to move from one job to another or to make business decisions as you please, but your lender doesn't care much about that. Regardless of who you work for, a part of your time will be dedicated to generating income to serve your debt to the lender.

Second, *it deprives you of future spending on the things you like*. If you buy a $20,000 car and finance it with a 5-year loan at a low 3.5 percent interest, you will have a monthly payment of around $400. You may accept the bank's argument that, because car loans are offered with low interest rates, this is a good deal that improves your cash flow for the next five years. Instead of cashing out the $20,000 now, you pay only $400 every month. But what you are never told is the fact that you will have to deal with a $400 payment every single month, money that you will have to pay unconditionally. Being a top priority (if you don't pay, you lose the car), this payment puts a hold on $400 per month of your future income, depriving you of other indulgences.

And this is applicable for every consumer good that you buy using credit. If you are in such a situation, just ask yourself a simple question—what could you do with the extra money if you did not have to pay your car payment today?

Leverage is nothing more than using other people's money (including bank loans) to amplify the outcome of your own investments. This means that if the investment decision is good and the investment leads to profit, leverage amplifies the positive outcome of the investment. But the reverse is also true—if the investment decision proves to be bad, leverage amplifies the negative outcome of the investment. In other words, you don't just mess up. You mess up big time. For instance, buying a rental property and financing it with a mortgage is, in most cases, a "good debt"—simply because tenants pay it off. Of course, we assume that property produces positive cash flow—which means that units are occupied and the rent covers all expenses related to mortgage, operating expenses, and taxes. The idea behind this is that every single month, the owner's equity in the property increases while someone else (the tenant) is paying to reduce debt. Robert Kiyosaki, in his book *Rich Dad's Cash Flow Quadrant*, explains this difference. He says,

> "Rich dad did borrow money, but he did his best to not become the person who paid for his loans. He would also explain to his son and me that good debt was debt that someone else paid for you, and bad debt was debt that you paid for with your own sweat and blood" (p. 205).

The idea that you can invest in productive assets using loans is reasonable. After all, you can expect that investment's return to exceed the interest you pay. Another thing you can expect is an appreciation of the value of the assets. Therefore, it seems like a good idea. The downside of this concept is that the asset value may be very volatile, fluctuating based on supply and demand, while the *debt* remains constant. There is always a chance of ending up in a situation where you have to service a loan, making constant payments, while revenues from the asset you purchased decrease to a lower level. Somehow, you will have to cover the difference from other sources or let the asset go out of your hands.

But maybe the most important advantage of a leveraged investment is the fact that *it makes it possible to pass on to the lender the negative effect of inflation*. If you make an investment using your own funds, inflation will take a cut of your return. For instance, if the return rate is 5 percent and the inflation rate is 2 percent, your real return on that investment is only 3 percent. But if a significant part of the investment represents loans, that loan is devalued with the same rate. In other words, the 2 percent inflation rate will reduce your return, but at the same time it will also reduce your loan with the same rate—meaning a 2 percent gain. In total, you will still keep your 5 percent return.

If there is a question why the rich get richer, here is one of the answers: wealthy people are able to access bank loans with low interest, and they use that money to make investments and maintain a high rate of return. They pass the negative effect of inflation onto the bank. On the other hand, the bank doesn't care much about it, because it creates money out of nothing using fractional reserve mechanism anyway or passes over this effect onto depositors—the people who save. The savers are the ones who finally pay the price of inflation.

Because leverage amplifies the outcome of the investment, positive or negative, it is important to observe that wealthy people use leverage only in connection with business investment, and are usually fully protected by a corporate structure. Thus, they make sure they do not incur any form of personal liability in connection with the investments they carry out. They are fully aware that lenders may change their policies overnight, and this can totally turn everything upside down in a matter of days. Therefore, in case of dramatic changes, a corporation can go bankrupt without affecting personal finances.

When Managing Your Personal Debt, Financial Discipline Is More Important than Formulas

Much good advice is out there on how to build wealth or, as a first step, to be free from the bondage of debt. Very often, people wonder what is the right approach for solving a particular problem, especially when they hear opinions that seem to contradict each other. For instance, if you have decided to pay off your entire debt using the "snowball method" (where you focus on paying off one debt a time), one opinion says that you should pay first the debt with highest interest rate. Mathematically speaking, this makes sense because you address first the debt that comes with the highest interest costs. The second opinion says that you should first pay off the debt with lowest balance, and the reason to do so is that eliminating one debt from your list, even a small amount, has a strong positive psychological impact, giving you the strength to move ahead through the process and making it possible to see the light at the end of the tunnel.

Both approaches can be correct or wrong—all depending on how you act. They key issue here is not the approach, but your *discipline*. If you are disciplined and manage to keep to your payment schedule as you planned, any of the approaches will work just fine and you will be debt free earlier than you thought. But if you do not control your spending habits, no formula will help.

This applies also to similar questions, such as, "Should I consolidate all credit card debt with a home equity loan?" or "Should I transfer a balance from one credit card to another to take advantage of the zero percent introductory offer?" As mentioned, in all these cases, and in others like it, *discipline is the key*. There are many things that mathematically make sense and are correct; after all, debt and interest are just simple percentage calculation and addition. But if you take action in one direction or another and still lack self-control, things will not get better; after a while you may even end up in a worse situation than you were before you started.

Insurance

I mentioned many things about being prepared for the unexpected when I analyzed savings, saying that the purpose of savings is to allow you to live without affecting your living standard for six months, in case an unfortunate event occurs. This is very important, and if you have these savings, it's good. But having savings will only allow you to continue living for a while, without any compensation for the damages caused by the particular event.

This is the role of insurance—to replace the value of something that is lost or destroyed.

Wealthy people create a foundation for their life so that when the unexpected occurs, they do not have to take extreme measures to help themselves or get help to get them out of the situation. It is good to be positive and optimistic and it is good to have faith in divine protection and believe that everything will go well; still, nobody is guaranteed a trouble-free life.

In addition to the emergency fund, wealthy people play their games wisely and build a foundation of assets that gives them the possibility of reacting without having to accept bad deals because they are forced to. They take risks and understand that risks and rewards go hand in hand. But they are always calculated risks and always within reasonable limits; this is possible because preparation reduces risk. Wealthy people develop strategies so they never end up in a paint-themselves-in-a-corner situation where, in order to escape, they are forced to accept unreasonable conditions.

As the main rule, insurance should cover everything connected to life and health, income sources, assets, and possessions. Without going into details, I will mention that all your insurances can be grouped into four main categories:

- *Life:* life insurance, wills;

- *Income:* disability, health, long-term care;

- *Assets:* business (including liability and malpractice, if applicable), real estate, other income-producing assets;

- *Possessions:* home, auto, and liability.

As this is a vast and complex area with many legal aspects, all advice should be given by insurance specialists and, especially when it comes to wills and trusts, attorneys.

Insurance is important, because wealth is not only about obtaining wealth, it's also about maintaining it once it's made.

PART II

The Non-Financial Resources Available to Anyone

Chapter 6
Creativity

Wherever you are at any given moment in your life, whatever you can see, feel, taste, smell, and hear, is a direct result of *creativity*. Even as you sit indoors comfortably reading this book, you can behold your surroundings, whether you are on a train or plane, at the library or bookstore, in a coffee house or a room located in a house, and know that this place was once was created by an architect and built by a contractor. Both architect and contractor used materials and tools that were somebody's *idea*. A furniture manufacturer used tools and materials created by somebody else in order to produce the couch, armchair, and bookshelf. The picture hanging on the wall was painted by an artist who released his or her creativity in a visual manner. The same applies to the background music that you to listen to—a song that was a composer's idea, arranged into sounds with instruments that were created by somebody else and played now on a gadget manufactured by a completely different person. Even the background noise that is due to the traffic generated by cars was created based on ideas.

And I can continue with many examples, understanding that, in fact, everything in our life is a direct or indirect result of a creative process. An idea was generated in order to solve a problem, and using what was available at that moment, that idea led to the creation of something new. *The Merriam-Webster Dictionary* defines creativity as "the ability to make new things or think of new ideas." Since the early beginnings of humanity, creativity has been one of the most important drivers of progress. Every improvement or change in society was brought forward as result of an idea.

The result of creativity is an external manifestation of something that comes from within. Although we can understand that some people are more creative than others, we can agree that creativity manifests in one form or another in each of us. Creativity is the native gift or talent that lies in each person; rephrasing this, we can say that we are the carriers of our own gifts, talents, and abilities. As I mentioned in my introductory chapter, there is a difference between *making* and *creating*. While making has its output from something that existed before, creating is about bringing forward something that did not exist before. Donny Deutsch, in his book *Big Idea*, explains,

> Big ideas are all around us. Every day I meet people who have come up with innovations that nobody ever thought of before. In each case, the idea grew out of a need, something that was missing, a frustration, the desire to make life a little easier, a little better. These are slap-yourself-on-the-side-of-the-head, obvious ideas. But it took people with the desire and motivation to see them through.

Unfortunately, society does little to encourage creativity in individuals. Most of us have been programmed to get an education and then get a job. This is why most people settle for less than what they are able to do. They look for a *job* instead of looking for *a place where they can release their creativity and use their abilities and skills*. Here are a few more things to say about creativity.

First, there is a connection between *creativity* and *having fun*. Having fun at work is not about turning your workplace into a sitcom site, but about enjoying every single minute of the time spent there. Being immersed in creative work gives you added energy; you become oblivious to how quickly the time passes, and the day finishes before you know it. But if you do not get involved, that is, release your creativity, every minute of work seems like torture . . . you look forward to the weekend and dread Monday mornings. Unless you start releasing the creativity within you and start using your native gifts and talents, it's impossible to have fun at work.

Second, your ability to be creative and innovative will also allow you to mark your *signature in life* - be it in science, arts, politics, architecture, business, or sports. Those remembered and honored today for their influence are people who generated something that made a real difference. Whatever they created represents their signature in life and makes them recognizable.

Picasso was ridiculed by his contemporaries because nobody had ever painted a portrait with eyes on the side of the face. But he replied, "I paint objects as I think them, not as I see them." And this was his signature in life. While his paintings are today displayed in museums and sold for millions at different auctions, nobody remembers his critics. Every time you turn the light on, you see Thomas Edison's signature in life—he was the one who created the electric bulb. When you say "Paris," you most probably think about the Eiffel Tower—the signature of the French architect and engineer Gustave Eiffel. When the creator of the *Harry Potter* series was asked, "How do you like to be remembered?" by journalist James Runcie on the TV documentary *J. K. Rowling—A Year in the Life*, she answered: "As someone who did the best with the talent she had."

Third, creative work is the only way mankind can sustain physical and financial life on this planet. You can argue that much creativity has been used for destruction—which is also true. When greed, hatred, and desire to control take over human character and behavior, the underlying gift of creativity will be used for evil—and this should not happen. Still, much more has been done for human progress and well-being than for destruction.

Fourth, creativity is an essential part of work. Most of the time, when you think of "work," you think about being active or busy. But being active or busy does not guarantee results or a desired outcome. Running on a treadmill is good as long as it serves its purpose—to consume calories and burn fat—but it doesn't take us anywhere. The key is the *outcome* of the effort. Therefore, work is about producing, and this is directly or deeply connected to creativity; you should see work as a force that is released in a creative form.

Fifth, creative work will increase your self-esteem and well-being. When you are working creatively, you turn yourself into a valuable asset for your employer, business, community, and society in general. Knowing that you are able to bear your own burdens and not be a burden to society will increase your self-esteem and self-worth. You will feel better, and it will be easier to maintain your health. On the other hand, boredom leads to depression and low self-esteem, which threaten your general well-being. Stress begins to take over, and in time, your general health may deteriorate.

Sixth, creativity will ensure your long-term employment. Creativity enables you to become more engaged and able to see the big picture as well as view situations from a higher perspective. You understand the meaning and purpose in the things you do, and when you are connected to something bigger than yourself, you find new resources to put into it. When you become completely engaged, retirement becomes no real option.

Wasting Creativity

What does it mean to waste creativity? Of course, it means to reject or refuse to develop or implement good ideas. But let us explore other ways of wasting creativity.

You waste creativity when you do not use your gifts and talents. Individual creativity is defined by the gifts and talents residing within each of us. Your wealth depends on the way and the extent to which your gifts and talents are used. Like a seed that contains all the characteristics of the plant it is to become, personal gifts and talents represent the seed containing the essence of your wealth.

A company that provides you a job cannot be the source of wealth, like ground alone cannot produce plants. In the same way as ground is the right environment for a seed to grow and become a plant, a job is just an environment where these gifts and talents can be developed and released. Not using your gifts and talents means you simply do everything in the way you were told to do. No personal touch and no variation—just like mass production machinery that releases the same product over and over again.

How do you find your gifts and talents? In his sermons and books related to achieving your life's potential, Dr. Myles Munroe revealed that you can find them by asking yourself three basic questions. Here's my take on the answers.

1. What do I do with ease?

Many things come naturally for any of us. Some are good with sports, some with math. Others sing or dance. The things you do with ease are always revealed in your childhood, but for some reason, while growing up, you were forced into a standardized system that inhibited any form of individuality. It may have been the school system, the corporate world, or even your own family that discouraged you in the process of becoming who you are supposed to be. The things you easily do are a good indicator of your gifts and talents.

2. What would I rather be doing?

When you are stuck in a job that you hate, you should ask yourself: "What would be that thing I would like doing if money weren't an issue?" In other words, if somebody else would take care of all your bills, what would you rather be doing? The things you like doing are also a good indicator of your gifts and talents.

3. What makes me angry?

It is easy to observe that life is not always fair, and it's not hard to identify something that can be changed for the better. In some areas, you find that things are so bad that you get angry. Other people may think that it's okay, but you don't. Your inner anger at the status quo is a signal that you can do something about it and make it better. Mother Teresa started out as an English teacher when she first arrived in India. But after a short while, during a train trip from Calcutta to Darjeeling, she noticed the conditions the poorest of the poor were living in. The inner anger and desire to help made Sister Teresa become the respected Mother Teresa we all know and admire.

But I will propose that just discovering your own gift is not enough. As every single person on this Earth is created with a specific gift, each has the responsibility of developing this gift to the level of mastering it—and using it to create a significant impact in the world. It is difficult to make a difference, have influence, or create an impact without mastering one's gift. People who are recognized as influencers in their field, be it science, arts, or sports, understand this principle. The great scientist Albert Einstein recognized the importance of talent in his life, saying, "The gift of fantasy has meant more to me than my talent for absorbing positive knowledge." The German writer Goethe said, "The person born with a talent they are meant to use will find their greatest happiness in using it." And Oscar Wilde: "I put all my genius into my life; I put only my talent into my works."

The combination of *creativity* and *use of gifts and talents* (abilities) generates power in your life, making it possible to take your efforts to the next level. If you do not use your gifts and talents, you lose the chance to generate that power. Professionals who can provide both creativity and skills are in such demand that they can write their own ticket in life; they are able to work and provide services on their own terms and not settle for less than what they are worth.

You waste creativity when you do not believe in your own ability to develop your ideas. Your brain is constantly receiving information. Everything you perceive with your five senses (sight, hearing, smell, touch, and taste) is processed by your brain and sorted into relevant and irrelevant information. While the irrelevant information is ignored, the information considered to be relevant is taken into consideration for further evaluation or action.

Creativity transforms your brain into an innovative mind that gives you progressive revelation and understanding. No piece of information submitted to a creative process will remain stagnant. Bill Bartmann says in his book *Billionaire—Secrets to Success*, "Self-belief is a product of the information we receive from our mind when we request information concerning our ability to accomplish a certain task." (p. 28)

Creativity means *thinking*. We humans were given a brain to use for thinking. There is always a better way to do the things we do. If you keep doing what you have always done, you will keep getting what you have always gotten. Albert Einstein defined *insanity* as "doing the same thing over and over and expecting different results." So every day you should be thinking of something new or at least trying to discover a way to make your life better. You become mentally lazy when you do not use your creative mind. As a result, you will never see any form of increase in the value of your current possessions.

If you are unwilling to manifest what is inside of you—an idea, a dream—it will die unborn. Every single day you kill ideas without even being aware of it. You may continually look for knowledge and wisdom, but when you have the opportunity to allow your own ideas to be part of that wisdom, you quit, killing and essentially burying the idea because you do not believe it is achievable, thus keeping it from being all it could have been. Will Smith, one of the most highly regarded actors in Hollywood, said in one of his interviews, "I believe that I can create whatever I want to create if I can put my head onto it right, study it and learn the patterns." The same idea is also supported by Oprah Winfrey who, in her video *Inspiring Words from Oprah Winfrey*, said,

> There are many laws working in the world. But it is very true that the way you think creates reality for yourself. There are other factors going on, so it's not everything, but you can really change your reality based on the way you think.

137

You waste creativity when you say, 'Somebody else must have done it before.' Sometimes the most innovative ideas can be found in the most ordinary places. It seems like miracles are passing us by every single day, but we either ignore them or think that they are so obvious that surely someone must have already implemented or tried them before. I'm sure you have had, at least once, a great idea cross your mind, an idea that had never been implemented before. An idea that seemed both obvious and simple . . . yet you didn't put it to work. It seemed like an excellent idea, but nothing was done to develop it or bring it to fruition. And you were okay with abandoning that idea until you discovered, some time later, that your idea was now a hot new product being sold on a late-night infomercial or even headlining the news. You realize that someone else birthed what you buried and is reaping the financial rewards of *your* idea. Does it really help to get mad and jealous? For sure many were thinking, before 2005, that there was a need for people to share on the Internet their own homemade videos. But three guys (Chad Hurley, Steven Chen, and Jawed Karim) decided to do something about it. They created a website where people could do exactly that—upload their (most often) junk movies so others could watch them. They called it *YouTube* and launched it officially in November 2005. One year later, in October 2006, *YouTube* was purchased by Google for $1.65 *billion.*

You waste creativity when you do not realize the full potential of your ideas. In our rush for quick results and instant gratification, we have a tendency to forget the power of *long-term potential.* Therefore, we abandon good ideas because we do not take the time to discover a way to put them into practice and to grow them step by step into businesses.

The potential of your ideas is stored as *unseen wealth.* This wealth is released only when something is done with the ideas. Putting ideas into practice will generate value, and as long as people are willing to pay for something they believe is valuable, your wealth is generated. But as long as the *potential* of your ideas is hidden, there is a great chance that it remains untapped. An idea is like a seed. Most seeds are small and weak. There is no challenge in crushing them with our fingers. But the same seed contains the potential of a great tree. All that it takes to transform a weak seed into a strong tree is *time* and the *right environment*. Tyler Perry, the successful playwright, producer, actor, and director, said in one of his interviews,

> Never despise small beginnings. There are things that can change the world and that can happen out of the smallest start.

The potential of your ideas is an *unused resource*. Any good idea that is developed into a business practice with excellence will attract resources. As many as there are entrepreneurs looking for funding, there are resourceful people looking to place their money into good businesses. In addition to financial returns, people are always drawn to reputable companies and businesses. Potential, if not sustained by creative work, will eventually end in poverty. The question isn't whether or not *you* have potential, because there is potential in each of us. The question is how much of *your* individual potential is achieved through releasing your creativity on this Earth. In his sermons, Dr. Myles Munroe repeatedly said,

> The graveyard is the richest place on Earth, because it is here that you will find all the hopes and dreams that were never fulfilled, the books that were never written, the songs that were never sung, the inventions that were never shared, the cures that were never discovered, all because someone was too afraid to take that first step, keep with the problem, or determined to carry out their dream.

Millions of people go through life filled on the inside with an abundance of treasures, yet nothing is released. It is like refusing to show up on the planet with what you have to share, and instead, being complacent, living an average life, going to an average job, getting an average paycheck, living in an average house, and being buried with an average tombstone that nobody notices when passing by.

You waste creativity when you maintain a 'job mentality.' Most people hate their jobs. According to Gallup's 2013 State of the American Workplace Report (http://employeeengagement.com/wp-content/uploads/2013/ 06/Gallup-2013-State-of-the-American-Workplace-Report.pdf), which surveyed 150,000 workers (both full- and part-time), only 30 percent of employees are engaged and inspired at work. This leaves 70 percent who do *not* feel engaged at work. Of those, approximately 52 percent are unhappy and disengaged—which leads us to suspect that Monday is the worst day of their entire week. They are present, but most likely desire to be somewhere else. The remaining 18 percent are those *actively* disengaged. These are the people who, according to Gallup CEO Jim Clifton, "roam the halls spreading discontent" (page 4). In other words, almost one out of five employees works actively to spread complaints and generate a negative, hostile environment. They keep themselves busy acting out their unhappiness and their resentments against their engaged coworkers' accomplishments and promotions. They are constantly thinking about leaving, and through the whole process, they remain frustrated until something else comes along. And this process continues nonstop. A disengaged mindset will rarely achieve a better life. Beyond statistical percentages, the figures related to financial losses are indeed scary. The same Gallup report indicated that actively disengaged employees cost the US up to $550 billion annually in lost productivity.

Abhorrence for work is the main cause of boredom in modern society. Most people do not have fun or take pleasure in what they are paid or employed to do. Certainly, for these people, there is absolutely no desire or appeal to prepare on Sunday night for the upcoming week. Moreover, there is no lingering excitement that compels them to want to wake up on a Monday morning ready and eager to put in eight to ten productive hours of work that will release their inner creativity. They are plagued with having a "job mentality"; that is, they see their job as just an occupation, an activity that takes up their time. It keeps them busy without any guarantee for efficiency. They are simply maintaining a task or doing the bare minimum to get through the day. For a person with a job mentality, the only motivator is the paycheck. People motivated only by the paycheck will always live a life in fear of losing the little they have. They are not connected to the company, they are not connected to what they do; they are just connected to their paycheck.

Unfortunately, when money is the only motivator, there is little possibility of a great future. As I noted in my first chapter, money is an *image of perceived value*. Money can be a means to an end, good or evil, but money can never be the end itself. Therefore, making money without a purpose is nonsense. Working for money alone is a dead end. It is like spinning wheels in a ditch—it uses lots of energy (gas), the engine revolves like when driving 100 miles per hour, but it's still not going anywhere. On the other hand, a creative work mentality focuses on achieving results and accomplishing objectives to bring a not-yet-seen vision into reality. It may be a personal vision or someone else's, but the motivation is to bring that vision into reality, not the need for a paycheck. We, all humans, have the *creative work mentality* within us. The question is whether we manage to let it manifest and grow and not allow a *job mentality* to suppress it.

While a job mentality keeps you *em*ployed, the creative work mentality gives you *de*ployment and allows you to take action—you become empowered and begin to work in the realm of inspiration and intuition. It offers endless possibilities to develop your knowledge as you start understanding how things work. Knowledge and creativity are always linked to each other.

A job mentality will cause you to complain about how long the days are. You see time passing very slowly because you find no enjoyment in being at work. But just think how quickly time flies when you are doing something you love to do! Having a meaningless job, you cannot wait to leave. Doing something meaningful and creative, you cannot wait to get there, and the time disappears. Most people come to their job late and leave as early as possible. But when they do what they love to do, nobody needs to remind them to show up on time, and they are usually the last to leave. So, when you have an unfulfilling and what seems to be a meaningless job, you cannot wait to leave; but when you are doing something fulfilling, meaningful, and creative, you cannot wait to get to work—you are oblivious to time.

It is important to understand that, once developed, a creative work mentality has to be maintained. Too often, people start off motivated and show strong engagement and commitment, but then, somewhere in the process, they become disinterested and deflated. A creative work mentality is hard to maintain when associating with disengaged people or in an environment where creativity is not appreciated. Still, you should continually remind yourself of your personal commitment to higher standards and create a pocket of excellence in that environment, regardless of peer pressure or your colleagues' opinions and comments.

Also pertinent is your understanding that your creative ability is *permanent*, while a job is always *temporary*. The limited time aspect of a job is even more valid today than it was years ago. For decades, spending an entire lifetime in the same company was the rule rather than the exception. Nowadays, no one can count on safe employment; those kinds of jobs are few and far between. It is fully possible, and likely, that you will be laid off from a job, quit, or retire. *But you can never retire from your life's purpose, nor can anybody lay you off from it.*

You waste creativity when your abilities are not recognized. Creativity is a gift that resides in each of us, and we are the carrier of gifts, talents, and abilities. These are personal assets that should give us enough self-confidence in what we do so we can release all of it into the place we work. Many of us go around with the feeling of not being recognized for what we can contribute. Especially in the corporate world, people feel that they represent just pieces in a big machine, controlled by procedures, checklists, and control routines. Or a fish in a big pond or ocean . . . never being noticed or recognized.

You have to understand the connection between *value* and *recognition*. Because people pay much attention to value, they appreciate only things considered to be valuable. Therefore, if you want to be given more recognition, you have to make sure that you bring value to the table. As long as you are sure that you add value, lack of recognition shouldn't be a major problem for you. If people do not appreciate what you deliver, this will be *their* problem.

Being involved in many different roles in a business environment, I fully comprehend the reasoning behind corporations' desire and efforts to implement "idiot-proof" policies and procedures. Still, in doing so, they do themselves a great disfavor. First, they make it easier for insecure and incompetent people to climb the corporate ladder and end up in a comfortable middle management seat. As a rule, these people are the most eager to do it, because they have an inner need to prove something. Once they get there, all efforts will be aimed not at improving operations but at pleasing superiors and doing whatever it takes to cover up for personal incompetence— especially frustrating subordinates with micromanagement and meaningless requests. The second consequence is that any creative person will end up behaving like an idiot, as the system does not allow for any form of individual action outside the agreed procedures.

Therefore, you should always look for places where there is room for growth and where your skills can be used. You should not stay in a place where you are imprisoned and your talents are buried. Still, this does not mean you should quit immediately when you do not see signs of recognition. You should stay in place as long as there are ways to learn and gain experience. Your confidence should come from the fact that your skills and talents will follow you when you leave the place. Your place is always in an environment where you can excel, and this is what you should look for.

You waste creativity when there's no passion in what you do. When you go to a place of employment where you hate what you do, all your efforts are meaningless. But finding what you love to do and pursuing it will suddenly make everything meaningful. Donny Deutsch, the host of the popular CNBC show *The Big Idea with Donny Deutsch*, explains in the introductory chapter of his book *Big Idea*,

> No matter what you do, if you are not passionate about it, find something else. I have never met a truly successful person who was not fired up about their work. [. . .] These guys have so much money, they don't have to work another minute of their lives. They work because it turns them on (p. 9).

Steve Jobs said in an interview,

> People say that you need to have passion in what you do. And it's so true, because if you don't, any rational person would give up. [. . .] And you have to do it over a sustained period of time. [. . .] Those successful are those who loved what they did, so they could persevere when things got really tough. While those who didn't love it, quit. (*www.youtube.com/watch?v=KuNQgln6TL0*).

This is also supported by Warren Buffett, who said in a *YouTube* interview with Steve Forbes,

> You have to do what you love, and it doesn't get any luckier than that. [. . .] I am 80 years now; I would be doing what I do now and I would have done the same in the past, even if the payoff should have been in sea shells or shark teeth or anything else. Every morning I go to work, I tap dance on the way there because every day is exciting. That's luck to me. (*www.youtube.com/watch?v=OF4JCmqF6ec*).

You waste creativity when you contemplate your previous achievements. We work hard to achieve something, and the feeling of success is indeed wonderful. Still, we can be trapped in our own successes. There is nothing wrong in being excited about a past achievement, but all your past achievements should be seen only as stepping-stones allowing you to move ahead and take things to the next level. Sometimes your success can be so overwhelming that you forget about moving ahead. Although you may have every reason to be proud and enjoy what you've done, it should not mean more than what it is—a meal that has been eaten already. Every single day you should ask yourself: "What am I going to achieve and create today so I can take things to a higher level?"

Spending Creativity

Times and circumstances might appear when you have to trade in your creativity. I have described in the previous section the ways or situations when you waste your creativity. Of course, doing the opposite of what was described means that we do not waste creativity—we spend it or invest it. As a principle, you can relate the idea of *spending creativity* to circumstances where you have to trade in your creativity in exchange for something. And one of the most obvious circumstances is when you are in an employee position. Most of the things said when describing the difference between creative work and job mentality apply to the situations where you receive a paycheck for your efforts.

You should always remember that, in addition to money, you receive tremendous opportunities to learn and gain experience. If you combine this with the fact that creativity is a flow, where the more you release, the more inspired you become, you will really understand the real value of a place of employment—as the place where you can be prepared and equipped for the journey into your own business.

Sometimes you are forced to spend creativity when it is obvious that a traditional organic growth model of a business cannot be applied to take things to a higher level. In order to grow, some businesses require a quantum leap—a major step ahead in terms of volumes and business scale that is not possible with resources available or that can be gathered normally. Many entrepreneurs are forced to sell their businesses because the investors considered a buyout to be the best option. This is a hard fact to face, especially for a business owner, because a business built from scratch feels like one's own child. And if there seems to be no clear answer for what's best to do, sometimes it's good to sell, because it's the only chance for the business to survive. Or, on the contrary, sometimes it may be better to keep it, because those who take over may close it in a few years anyway.

Another typical situation of spending creativity is when you directly sell an idea while it's still an idea. It may even have been granted a patent or a trademark, but it takes way too much for you, as creator, to develop it into a sellable product or service. Selling it to an investor or entity that has the capacity to take it to the market is the only way to make use of that idea.

There are also many examples of people whose true gift is *innovation*. They are able to create new things, and their ideas may even be at a genius level; still, they are not gifted as entrepreneurs. When trying to build a business based on their idea, there is a big chance of failure—not because the idea is not valuable, but because they don't have the skills to build and run a business based on that idea. It may take some courage to admit one's own limitations, but in this case, the best solution is to focus on the true gift—continue to innovate and generate new ideas and sell them to people who can build businesses. In all these situations, creativity is used to get something else in exchange—money, experience, acknowledgment — something that you can later use as an *asset*.

Investing Creativity

Having learned what it means to *waste* and *spend* creativity, let us now see how to *invest* creativity—releasing it in order to generate a future flow of benefits.

You invest creativity when you put work behind your ideas. We always say that money is important, and we even feel that we value money. But in fact, we value money only if we value *work* as a means to acquire it. Money acquired without work is not valued, and people who do not value money end up spending it very quickly. In our constant rush for instant gratification, we'd prefer to reap the fruit of somebody else's labor rather than growing our own crop. But regardless of how smart we are, nothing will happen in our lives until we make it happen.

No matter what they say, politicians will never do anything to make people wealthy. At most, they will speak about "creating" jobs—so they do not have to deal with the negative outcomes of unemployment. But the jobs they create will never bring wealth, because no real value is generated. The government-created jobs will just keep people busy and help them to live paycheck to paycheck as long as funds are available. If you rely on this kind of created job, poverty will continue to remain in your life, and you will have to deal with it until you decide to do something about it.

Just showing up at a place of employment will not cause you to be recognized. You are appreciated when you combine *creativity* and *skills* (skills that you have developed through *time* and *effort*) in a way that they can be easily recognized and distinguished. You are appreciated when you are willing to go the extra mile and when you prove to have a higher level of understanding of the things you have to deal with on a daily basis. As a self-test, you should ask yourself: "Do I look forward more to the weekend than to the week?" If the answer is "yes," this means that you see your activity as a job, not as *work*. If you really love what you do, you should not want to break for the weekend. From this perspective, the weekend would simply be an interruption in your creative work.

The only reason to stop working is to restore energy. If you see work as a form of releasing creative energy, you need time to step back, so you can restore it. It is like driving a car on a long journey, when you stop once in a while to fill the tank and let the engine cool down. If you don't stop, you will run out of gas in the middle of the road and be unable to continue. As it should be in your life, rest is necessary to rejuvenate yourself and to restore your energy so you can continue the process of releasing creativity.

Any dream that is not backed by a willingness to work to fulfill that dream will remain only a dream, only a fantasy. So many times you have dreams, but you seldom move from the dream stage to realization. Dreaming is exciting, but it takes engagement and commitment to bring it to fruition. There must be engagement for it to happen. Without work, there is no difference between a dream and a fantasy.

We also have to understand that miraculous financial prosperity does not happen without work. Prosperity in life will not happen by simply participating in financial seminars. Such seminars are excellent opportunities to learn, as long as they provide useful information, but results will come only after applying what was taught in the seminar. Neither does miraculous financial prosperity happen by sending a gift of money to a TV preacher who promises to send a piece of "anointed" cloth that is supposed to provide a "financially miraculous breakthrough." Individual prosperity comes as result of *creativity released from within and then put to work.*

You invest creativity when you make it a part of your destiny. Your creative attitude is mirrored in the way you conduct your life every single day and in every single situation; when used consistently, your creativity designs your life. Your engagement or disengagement is directly linked to the use of creativity, innovation, and skills on a daily basis. This will further determine the path in life on which you will journey. J. K. Rowling, the successful author of the *Harry Potter* series and first billionaire writer, explained in an interview with Oprah Winfrey: "I was not the world's most secure person. I was not a person with so much self-belief at all. But if there was one thing in my life I believed, it was this: that I could tell a story." Her creativity became a part of her destiny.

Investing creativity will protect you from difficult times. Combining *ideas* with *work* will enable you to be recognized and desired—because of your personal contribution, not because of legal requirements. The best workers are the last ones to be laid off. Even if the company goes under for some reason and the owner must close the company, who will he call first when he starts a new venture?

Being aware of potential pitfalls does not make you a pessimistic person. It is rather a matter of sound risk analysis, where you evaluate several things. First, you need to think about what can go wrong. Then, consider how great are the chances for that negative event to occur and what can be done to prevent it from happening. And, finally, if it happens, determine what the impact is and how it can be fixed. Donald Trump, in an interview for *Expanded Books* about his book *Think Like A Champion*, said,

> I have always believed in positive thinking. At the same time, I don't want to mislead. I also believe in aspiring to protect against the downside. You cannot be just this wonderful guy walking around like everything is positive because, unfortunately, this is not the way the world is. I love to tell people to think about challenges, so when challenges do come along, you are ready for them (*www.youtube.com/watch?v=6u]zZkgureo*).

You invest creativity when you make it a key factor to your success. We are tempted to evaluate success in life by money or by net worth, another monetary expression. But success is rather defined by how much creative work we generate. Success is not related to the amount of resources available to us, but what is done to create something new out of those resources. Many people have lots of resources available, yet they are not successful; they sit on those resources and do nothing.

Your workplace, regardless of whether it's a place of employment or a privately owned business, represents an environment where you can use your creativity and transform abilities into skills that allow you to rise to the next level. Many people make the mistake of believing that there should be a difference between being an employee and being self-employed or running your own business. The difference seems to be that, being employed, the employer is the only one reaping benefits of creativity. But in fact, he is not. Creativity is a flow—the more you release, the more inspiration you get. Therefore, releasing creativity is a good habit, and there is no better place to start practicing it than as an employee. It is like good paid training, knowing that as you practice, greater things will come. Nobody describes this idea better than Oprah Winfrey, who, when talking about herself and her life, said,

> Had I not been on TV and were I working in a shoe store someplace, I do believe that I would be the person who would be selling the most shoes [. . .] because people would come around and have the conversations that we would be having while they tried on the shoes. I never imagined that I would be sitting and talking to you all on television. [. . .] Whatever you believe you were born to do, you do it—find a way to allow the truth of yourself to express itself. [. . .] Unless you are doing that, unless you find the way for what you believe to be true about yourself, to express and manifest itself in the world, you are not living the fullest life.

You invest creativity when you become a producer. The entire world's population is divided between producers and consumers, where producers represent less than 10 percent of the total. That means, on average, out of ten people, only one produces goods and services, and the remaining nine pay for them. *A person's growth in life will always be connected to their ability to produce.* Is it any wonder some people have more than others and some people accumulate wealth while others don't?

Manufacturers make products that people are buying. Service providers offer services that people are paying for. Musicians produce songs people pay to listen to. Moviemakers create movies that people pay to watch. The same applies to athletes who play a sport. Every time you take money out of your pocket, whatever you pay for, a part of it goes to the *producer*—directly or indirectly. Of course, you can argue that "we cannot all be producers; somebody must consume what is produced." This is very true, but the question is, why shouldn't it be *you* among the ones who produce and reap the fruit of *your* creation?

Creative and productive people will always be in great demand because of their skills. Therefore, if you want to be in demand, you should do your best to become skillful at what you do. A person in demand will never be unemployed. Good people are never laid off. And even if the company is sinking, the boss will throw a life jacket to employees he really appreciates. Consequently, looking for a guaranteed, secure job is nothing more than *a cover for an inability to produce*. When your instinct for survival and need for safety prevail, you are scared of losing your job. But the real fear is not about losing a job that you hate to go to anyway. The real fear is that, once this job is lost, it will be very hard to find another one. Developing a *creative work mentality* will always diminish this fear, and you will be more secure knowing that, if you lose the job, you will always find another one, similar or even better.

You invest creativity when you provide solutions to problems. Money comes as a reward for solving problems. When you want money, you should not look for a place of employment where you can spend a little time (and in some cases waste time) and get a paycheck. If you just show up and hang around the water cooler watching the clock waiting to go home and are more excited about leaving than coming, then something is completely wrong. If you want money, *you should look for problems to solve.* You are hired to show up and

151

bring in your *creativity* and your *skills* to solve your employer's problems. Your paycheck is not an entitlement due to you because you are a human and have needs, but instead it is the reward or payment for problem solving, productivity, and added value.

You should spend your days being solution oriented, not problem conscious. Every problem has a solution built into it. The problem and the solution are like the head and the tail of a coin—they coexist and cannot be separated. But in order to see both sides of the coin, you need to have a standpoint outside the coin and be able to flip it. In the same manner, you cannot see the solution as long as you just look at the problem. You need to somehow, through gaining additional knowledge and understanding, rise above the problem. As Albert Einstein once said, "No problem can be solved from the same level of consciousness that created it."

Every single person who achieved success in a sustainable manner is a person who knew how to solve problems. Thomas Edison addressed the problem of darkness. He came with a creative idea and worked at it until he figured it out. Today we enjoy and even at times take for granted the convenience and ease of flipping on a light switch, not even being aware that Edison released creative energy to create the bulb. This is not to say that if he hadn't done what he did, we would still be lighting our houses with oil lamps or candles, because most probably somebody else would have invented the bulb in the meantime, but we still have to give Edison the credit for solving this problem.

You invest creativity when you show engagement. Engaged, creative employees work with passion and feel a profound connection to their place of employment. They possess drive and innovation, and with their skills they help their organization to move forward. They are always there to make an extra effort, and they are focused on a measurable outcome. Engaged, creative workers pursue the outcome and the satisfaction of a job well done, regardless of whether they receive recognition from supervisors or managers. They feel good when the day is over because they were productive and accomplished things. Their self-esteem is high and their purpose is fulfilled.

Engaged, creative workers are a company's strongest asset; therefore, they are valued by the company and searched for by the competition. Showing this kind of work ethic will always yield value. When you do not feel like the company is valuing you, it should be time to ask yourself: "What can I change before expecting the company to make a change?"

As I mentioned before, people pay more attention to value than anything else in the world, and only things that are valuable are recognized. Therefore, if you want to be given more attention, you must increase your value. Value, attention, and recognition go hand in hand.

You invest creativity when you transform the unseen into the seen. A creative work mentality acts like a transfer of energy. In the process of creation, you take something that does not exist in reality and release it into something new on this human planet. You enjoy the results of the process initiated by your creativity, and this energizes you; it makes you excited every morning when you start your day, because there is something that you can look forward to. And this process develops a spiral effect. This energy inspires you to continue releasing creativity. The more you create, the greater the satisfaction of accomplishment, something that leads to a new level of energy.

Chapter 7
Time

A quick examination of the way our society rewards individuals reveals that it is not always the fastest who win the races, it is not necessarily the strongest who win the battles, and many of the smart and really gifted are often poor. The obvious fact is that being fast, smart, strong, or talented is no guarantee of a successful life. Nor will education alone be a huge contributing factor. Why is that? Plain and simple, because winning, success, prosperity, and wealth relate, in most cases, to *timing*. And timing means two things: (1) efficient use of time and (2) being at the right place at the right time. Timing is essential when it comes to achieving and reaching our goals. Getting what we want from life always comes back to timing. With that said, we have to clarify that this chapter of this book is not about time *management*. Instead, what we'll do here is follow the stated philosophy—to view time as a resource and understand what it means to *waste, spend,* and *invest* it.

When observing the habits of wealthy people, it's apparent that one important factor that differentiates them from poor people is *how they value time*. I mentioned earlier that you always value what you believe to be important. Wealthy people regard time as very important; an imperative Thomas Edison recognized when he said, "Time is really the only capital that any human being has, and the only thing he can't afford to lose."

I also said in the previous chapter, when I analyzed creativity, that putting work behind your ideas is one of the ways your creativity is invested and produces returns. But this is only a part of the truth. It is also true that the manifestation of your dreams, desires, and progress, together with all good things you expect to see happening in your life, will, in addition to creativity, *take time*. So, given its importance, let us review some facts about time.

Fact #1: Time is endless, but we get it in manageable portions. Time is probably one of the most discussed and analyzed concepts in the history of philosophy. Many of the ancient philosophers, the medieval thinkers, illuminists, and modern scientists have dedicated their lives to finding out how we should understand and relate to time.

Our understanding of *eternity* as "something beyond time" is somewhat vague and can be both scary and too much to comprehend. However, *time*, when given in the form of days, months, years, or even decades and centuries, is much easier to grasp. Abraham Lincoln expressed this idea very well: "The best thing about the future is that it comes one day at a time."

Your entire lifetime is nothing but a collection of days. Your life is in *today* because *only today* can you do something about the direction of your future. And although sometimes you may really want to, you cannot revert to yesterday, nor can you operate in tomorrow. It may seem like a paradox—while you plan for tomorrow, you can act only in the moment today; thus, today, this very moment, is the beginning of your future.

Time is indeed endless. But you get it in manageable portions, and what you do today determines what happens tomorrow. If you make long-term plans for your life and put them into practice day by day, and make adjustments only to overcome challenges but not lose focus on where you are supposed to go (your final destination), you will be far less likely to utter the words "I wish I were young again."

How much time do we really have? Because time is given to us in manageable portions, we are used to thinking about it in a measurable way (minutes, hours, days, weeks, months, and years). But this may hinder us from getting a larger perspective on the actual amount of time we have available. If we assume 75 years as a typical lifetime on this planet, most of us will end up spending 15 total years (day and night) at work. That is the equivalent of 8 hours a day, 5 days a week, from the age of 22 to 65. Furthermore, 8 hours of sleep every night means a total of 25 years in bed. Spending two and a half hours every day for meals represents no less than 67,500 hours at the dinner table—which is the equivalent of around 8 years. The conclusion is that, out of a 75-year lifetime, you end up spending two-thirds of it (almost 50 years) working, eating, and sleeping. This gives you not more than 25 years for education and leisure time. Does this sound like too much? Not to me. The hard conclusion is that *you do not really have much time to waste*.

Fact #2: Time, like money, can be tracked. I stated earlier that wealthy people do not waste money. Therefore, the first, and a very important, step is to cut those expenses that represent waste. Before doing so, you need to track all your expenses and determine where your money goes. If you understand time as a resource that you receive and use, you can apply the same method of writing down, for a certain period, what you do with your time. Having a closer look at the way you spend your time will help you to understand where your life is headed. The presumption that your life is going the right way just by itself is not enough. You have to make sure that you are on the right course and in line with your commitments, goals, and objectives. This requires that you budget your *time* exactly as you would budget your *money*. As with finances, when you decide beforehand how much money you are going to use for different types of expenses, you decide in advance how you are going to allocate your time to different activities.

Fact #3: Your life can be found in the place where you spend your time. When you want to know more about somebody, one of the things you can do is to study their habits and see how they use their time. This is a good indicator, because a person's life can always be defined by where he or she spends the most time. If someone is spending all day at work, from 7 am to midnight, then it's safe to say that working is his life. When a man is dedicating much of his time to golf, turning his wife into a golf widow, his life is golf. For the guy spending more of his time with buddies than with his family, his life is with buddies. A teenager playing games on computers for more time than he spends studying has a life in computer games.

Choosing the activities and environments to which you dedicate time will determine, in the long run, the direction, progression, and growth of your life. Certainly, this is why wealthy people surround themselves with other wealthy people, discussing ideas and ways to increase their wealth. They do not surround themselves with poor-minded people. Why? Because their focus is about turning ideas into wealth, and they want to associate with people who share ideas about ways to grow. On the other hand, poor people keep company with poor people, and their conversations are always filled with complaints about being poor. The saying "misery loves company" may be true, but this should not be part of *your* life.

Fact #4: If you do not control your time, somebody else will. In his book *The Seven Habits of Highly Effective People*, Dr. Stephen R. Covey introduced the concept of the Time Management Matrix, in which two factors define an activity: its *urgency* (whether it requires immediate action or not) and its *importance* (meaning relevance for results). According to this concept, each activity can be included in one of the following four categories:

- urgent and important;

- not urgent, but important;

- urgent, but not important;

- not urgent and not important.

Urgency is the dominant force, and will always take control over your life. Therefore, the best way to control your time is to avoid ending up in circumstances of urgency, because, if not, urgent activities end up overtaking you. Life becomes a form of constant firefighting, where you run from one fire to another trying to put them out one by one. As soon as you manage to extinguish one fire, another one pops up in another area. Right prioritizing is not about urgency, but about *importance*. You should focus on activities based on their importance, addressing first the most important issues that have long-lasting solutions. In this way you will discover that you'll deal less and less with urgency. Taking control of your time is essential because, if you don't, someone else will.

Fact #5: We all have available the same amount of time. Every single person on this Earth has the same amount of time in a day—24 hours. If you ask the richest people on Earth what they wish they'd had more of, all would answer the same—more time. They can always buy a bigger house, they can always buy the latest car model, and they can buy all the clothes and shoes they want. Still, they are not able to extend their day by even a single minute. Unfortunately, lost time cannot be gained back. Once it's gone, it's gone forever. Sometimes you can catch up with delays, and it's true that it is never too late to do the right thing; still, none of these will ever bring back lost time. Knowing that not even Bill Gates or Warren Buffett has more time than you have available, you can ask yourself, "What do I do with the time I have?" The more efficiently you use your time, the more productive your life will be.

Fact #6: Time determines the seasons of life. Life consists of seasons, and your success depends also on how well you adapt to those seasons. You expect big things to happen, but your expectations are perhaps more like looking forward to winning a lottery ticket. There is a slight chance of winning, and if it happens, your life will be totally changed. But still, you must understand that expecting something good to happen requires that you prepare for it. Seen from this perspective, the seasons of life represent a series of adjustments. In order to move toward the place you want to be and away from the place you are, you have to make adjustments for those seasons. Although you have no guarantee of protection from the unexpected, this perspective allows you to design and plan for the future rather than living it from crisis to crisis.

We start our life journey as infants and grow into children, teenagers, and adults. Each of these stages requires different approaches and different levels of understanding. We grow in life, but the process of learning never ends. As we grow older, we move from one social level to another, we move from one financial level to another. Not always up—sometimes after an upturn comes a downturn. But understanding the seasons of life will help us to better deal with these changes, especially the downturns. In fact, the downturns are the times when we really grow and get stronger. We find new ways to access resources and dig for new reserves that we hadn't believed were available to us—somewhat like a tree that, in a dry season, is forced to stretch its roots deeper into the ground to find water and nourishment. With deeper and stronger roots, the tree will be able to flourish in the wet season.

Fact #7: Whatever you possess is purchased at the exchange of time. Everything that is in our possession today was once purchased with the price of time. You may think it was paid for with money. Sure, but how did we get that money? By being in a place of employment where we were paid a certain amount per hour. We put our time in, and the employer paid us accordingly. Or we took the time to manage a business that generated money.

You may say that was not just time, but also *skills*. Sure, but how did you acquire those skills? You put in time in school, and this helped you to acquire them. You also took time to develop the same skills over the years. Even when possessions are transferred from one generation to another, the older generation had to purchase them with time. Whatever you possess can be traced back to an amount of time that was spent to purchase it. This is why we say that *time is money*. Not just because time is valuable, which is true, but also because time acts like a currency.

Fact #8: Time is a revealer of true intent and hidden agendas. Time will reveal whatever there is on the inside of people. Your decisions are made at different moments, in different circumstances. Some of these decisions are extremely important to your life. It may be the choice of a spouse or a business partner; it may be a career choice or a major business decision. At any given moment and circumstance, the decision may seem to be the right one. Only the passing of time will reveal whether a decision was right or wrong. As time passes, circumstances may change and all commitments be put to a test. And only the passing of time will reveal whether the people whom you trust have honest intentions in building a relationship with you, or if they have a hidden agenda to take advantage of you and promote their own benefits.

Fact #9: Time is a key ingredient of any development process. Everything that is great, be it in nature or a major human achievement, is a result of a process that takes time. One of the basic laws that governs our universe is the law of sowing and reaping. We can witness it everywhere around us. But reaping a harvest can never be done immediately after sowing. A process that requires time (and also work) is involved, a process that enables you to collect the benefits of what you once sowed, but only if you patiently wait out the required time.

Modern society is based on instant gratification. Technology allows us to always be connected. If we request information, we expect to get it right away from a web page. When we take a picture, we can see the result directly on the display; we do not have to deliver the film to the lab and wait one hour for processing. We no longer send a letter and wait patiently for two weeks for a reply; we just send an e-mail or text message or even initiate instant messaging. Newer generations have a hard time imagining how things used to happen just few years ago. And this alone will cause lots of challenges, because not everything is subject to instant processing. Younger people who grew up surrounded by gadgets and devices will find it harder and harder to understand the importance of *time* and *process.* They will try to eliminate from their thinking almost everything that inherently implies waiting.

Therefore, comprehending the concept of a *process* will help create the winners of the future; those who have this understanding will patiently create and develop products and services that the majority, who lack the required patience themselves, will rush to buy. By understanding all the facts described above, it is logical to claim that time acts like the universal currency of a prosperous life.

Wasting Time

The statistics show that the vast majority of the population waste more time than they use wisely. And unfortunately, "wasted time is one of the biggest robbers of prosperity". Time is one of the most precious gifts you are given in life. But when you are unwilling to respect and protect it, you can sabotage the success it can bring to your life. As with other valuable things, if you do not respect time, it will simply disappear. When talking about wasted time, the first things to think about are the "time thieves"—those small habits that consume your time without any purpose.

Television is probably one of the worst time wasters of our day. According to a study performed by the Bureau of Labor Statistics in 2012 (*www.bls.gov/news.release/atus.nr0.htm*), the time spent in front of TV averages 2.8 hours per day. Most people end up wasting hours every evening sitting on a couch and being passive consumers, without realizing that the people they are watching on TV already got paid for their work. In other words, the producers and celebrities have already received their paychecks, while the viewers sit and are entertained by what others have produced. The more people watching, the more money they make. And every time there is a rerun, they make even more money. Many years from now, TV stars will still be making money and people will still be watching. The study also revealed that a person living the average expectancy of life will end up spending nine (!) years in front of the TV. The question is, what do they expect to get out of it? This does not mean that you should throw away the TV set. Instead, determine what you are learning from the programs you watch. How do they improve your life? A program without any educational value is a time thief.

Meaningless phone conversations also eat up your time. Modern technology makes it possible for us to be available anytime. This is a blessing, but also a curse. The phone is supposed to be used for the exchange of useful information, not for mindless discussions about nothing, driven by boredom or because you don't have something better to do. In addition, phones can be a distraction; this is because, typically, when the phone rings, it gets your top attention. It creates a sense of urgency because you feel that you have to attend to it. You get interrupted, you lose your focus, and your efficiency decreases significantly. You should manage the time spent on the phone and let calls go to voice mail whenever you are involved in important activities. As pointed out before, if you do not control your time, someone else will.

Amusement and entertainment beyond a reasonable limit represent other time thieves. Of course, entertainment has its role. After a long day or any long stretch of hard work, there is nothing better than to sit down, relax, and be entertained by others—for example, watching a comedy or a sporting event. Still, you need to prioritize and put these activities in the right perspective. Being amused and entertained is good, as long as it is done for the purpose of relaxing and recharging your batteries. In other words, you need to understand why you do it and put the right limitations on it. If entertainment and amusement exceed the "relax and recharge" level, it turns into a *waste*. Entertainment has two partners, the one who *produces* and the one who *consumes*. And the *consumer* is always the one paying for it. Therefore, being an *over*consumer of entertainment will bring limited, if any, benefits.

In addition to the time thieves mentioned above, let us now examine a few more scenarios for wasting time.

You waste time when you are lazy. As mentioned, we all need relaxation and recovery after a period of hard work. It's a legitimate need for your body. Still, there are limitations, and eventually excess rest will turn you into a lazy slug. You may have days when you are overly passive, and it is not always easy to admit it. As a rule, you will find all kind of excuses for not doing what you are supposed to do; if you are honest with yourself, you will eventually admit that laziness took ahold of you. Relaxation should be included as a priority activity in your schedule, keeping an adequate, predetermined ratio between work and rest.

You waste time in the presence of people who are constantly in a state of confusion. This may seem like a hard and selfish statement, but it is not. We are not talking about situations when good friends (who appreciate you and value you and your time) come to you asking for comfort, advice, or support during a difficult moment in their lives. We are referring to people who are "constantly confused." Certain unstable and immature people whose lives are a permanent mess are always in confusion and jump from one bad situation to another, playing the victim and having no inner desire for making a change. Their confusion makes them believe that they are entitled to consume your time with their dramas. If you value time and respect your own time, you should not allow someone else to disrespect it. Sooner or later you should understand that not everybody is qualified to consume your time. This may sound arrogant, but it's rather about being responsible. Your time is simply too valuable to allow somebody to draw you into their own life shows. As a matter of fact, it's worthwhile to note that people who disrespect your time will not have much respect for your *wisdom* either.

You waste time when you are around people who are constantly critical. Some people are constantly critical of everything and everybody. As a rule, they are people who have no dreams or purposes of their own, and therefore they have nothing else to do but second-guess everybody else's attempt to achieve something. They always have a negative outlook, focusing on what is not good enough; they never bring a constructive suggestion for improvement. The deeper the relationship, the harder it is for you to deal with their critiques. They may be dear friends, loved ones, or even members of your family, and your problem is that you spend more time trying to justify yourself to critics than you spend with people who believe in your dreams. This is a good reason for denying constant fault-finders access to your time.

You waste time when you try to help people who refuse to change. One of the quotes we hear very often (attributed to Francois de la Rochefoucauld) is "The only constant in life is change." Everything around us is changing; nothing is stagnant. Even the universe has been expanding continuously since it was created. Dynamics is a part of life, and we can see it everywhere—in nature, in society, in the economy.

As I noted when I talked about *seasons*, our understanding of changes and ability to adapt to them will determine our individual success. Some people refuse to accept this concept and remain blocked in their mentalities and traditions. Some traditions are good and important, as long as they represent the fundamental principles of life and are a part of our own identity. But beyond that, daily habits should be subject to change. We all know the proverb "Give a man a fish and you feed him for a day. Teach a man to fish and you feed him for a lifetime." It is a good principle, but it presumes that people in need *prefer* to learn to fish. Unfortunately, we meet people who reject this idea; they simply prefer to be given a fish today and will come back for another fish tomorrow. This kind of behavior, when people refuse to change their lifestyle, habits, or mentality and not adapt to new realities, disqualifies them from getting help. No matter how much you struggle, you will never be able to bring a change that goes against a person's own lack of desire or will to change. And even if you do, the result will not be long lasting; it will not be seen as necessary, and you will end up being blamed for all difficulties that occur later on.

You waste time when you fail to do something right the first time. The American basketball player and coach John Wooden, nicknamed the "Wizard of Westwood," once said, "If you don't have time to do it right, how will you have time to do it later?" Being under pressure or in a rush, we sometimes do not take the necessary time to learn how to do things right. Or we neglect to perform the small quality checks that ensure we are doing things the right way. Have you ever left home without checking to see if you had everything you need? I'll bet you have—wasted time making a trip back and looking for what you didn't find. Or when in the office, have you ever sent a document to the printer without checking the page layout, only to discover that you have to print it again (and it's just your luck that the printer runs out of paper exactly in that moment)? Have you ever wrapped and packed things not checking if you tightened caps and corks, just to have the contents running out of containers, so you have to clean, rewrap, and repack everything? I do not know about you, but this has happened to me many times . . . and of course, I can give you countless similar examples that you can also relate to. In one way or another, the end result was bad and you spent much more time (let alone money) on redoing the thing you had already spent time doing once.

You waste time when you are concerned about the task itself rather than its outcome. Although we understand the importance of planning what we have to do, we tend to focus too much on activities. We make elaborate to-do lists, but we do not pay enough attention to the results. Because everything you do should have a purpose, this clearly means that you should never engage in anything that doesn't have a purpose, and so you have to ask yourself what you want to achieve with a specific activity. Concentrating on the *outcome* of what you want to achieve will increase efficiency. One of the concepts in the field of project management states that each activity is finished with a deliverable—something that can be defined and measured in a quantitative and qualitative manner. And while you think about what you plan on doing, you have to make sure to define exactly what you expect to achieve with that activity: What is the outcome? Focusing on that outcome will help you make better use of your time, whatever you want to do. For instance, when calling and leading a meeting, you focus discussions toward the desired outcome, making sure you keep everybody on track and cut out any digressions that may occur.

You waste time when you are not organized. Mess produces waste. This is also valid for time. You waste time looking for things you do not find; you repeat doing things because you didn't finish what you started and the half-done part cannot be used. Maybe you rely too much on your memory, ignoring the fact that mistakes happen when you presume that you can remember everything. Thus, instead of you running an event, you end up being run by it. As a general statement, we do not realize that the main purpose of our mind is *creativity*, not memorizing. Memorizing is a good brain exercise, and we should keep doing it as an exercise. We use our minds for creativity, and we use tools to keep our information in order.

You waste time when you quit. Every time we start something, we wonder: "Am I going to succeed, or am I going to fail?" Fear of failure is one of the biggest obstacles to success. If you are not already aware of that, you need to realize that achieving success is a process that can contain some failures along the way. Robert Herjavec, successful entrepreneur and one of the investors in the popular TV program *Shark Tank*, said in one of his interviews,

> We try and fail. We fall down and rise again and try again. And we fail again. But just go on. Sometimes, the only difference between success and failure is the fact that we were able to stand one more time.

When the fear of failure starts growing inside of you, the feeling of panic takes over. Panic is always counterproductive, and it affects your ability to think and act. Additionally, your efficiency decreases and your creativity to find solutions is also blocked. Whenever you initiate something, you have to make sure that you make the necessary preparations, counting both risks and costs. This will equip you to better face the challenges and remain steadfast throughout the entire process.

Quitting is always an option. But you have to realize that whatever was done before quitting may be wasted. Even if you can resume the process later on, there is always a loss of momentum—which is a waste. So, being in the middle of a difficult time, the question to ask yourself is: "If I can quit anytime, why should I do it now?" Playwright, director, producer, and writer Tyler Perry, in one of his interviews, described his difficult start:

> I struggled from 1992 to 1998—there were six years of heartbreak, six years of doing the show while they didn't give me time off from work. So I had to quit the job, go out and do the show; I prayed out that it would work, but nobody showed up. In Birmingham, Alabama, it was so bad, the audience started to walk out in the middle of the show, complaining. That was the most horrible feeling. I had rushed, the cast wasn't ready, the sound was horrible, and that was probably the worst night I ever had on stage. I gave up in 1998 and had to be talked into doing one more show. Some friends called and told me "you should really do this one more show." And I told them "no." I kept losing my job, I got homeless, I was tempted to take my mom's advice to get a job making $300-400 a week and get some benefits. It would be great—this was her dream for me. I argued and yelled and cursed and screamed at friends . . . But finally I agreed to do that one show on March 12, 1998, at the House of Blues in Atlanta . . . and that changed my life. Sold out.

Resisting the temptation to quit was also the main reason that J. K. Rowling is today the first billionaire writer. Being turned down by no fewer than twelve editors who did not believe that *Harry Potter* would become a success, she explained in one of her interviews with Oprah Winfrey,

> Why do I talk about the benefits of failure? Simply, because failure meant the stripping away of the inessential. [. . .] It is impossible to live without failing at something unless you live so cautiously that you might as well not have lived at all. [. . .] We don't speak about failure enough. We speak about success all the time and I've been so fortunate to meet so

many extraordinary people through *Harry Potter*, not one of them didn't have their failures. The ability to resist failure or use failure is what often leads to the greatest success.

You waste time when you live in fantasyland. Wealthy people do not read many fantasy novels. They may do it once in a while, but when they do, there is always a purpose behind it. They may want to expand their vocabulary or ability to express themselves; they may want to improve their skill to describe visually their ideas using words, or simply just to relax. Wealthy people do not waste time living in fantasyland. Big dreams are important, but when there is no action behind them, the dream is just an escape from reality, and there is no benefit from it. You should take your dream, focus on what you have to start with, and set up a plan to make the dream a reality.

You waste time when you indulge in self-defeating habits. Self-defeating habits are those things that may start in an "innocent" way, but that little by little take control of your life to the point of self-destruction. Indulging in any form of self-defeating habit (e.g., alcohol abuse, smoking, drugs, gambling) steals your joy and peace; it kills your self-esteem and self-worth. A self-defeating habit has no future in it, and therefore is a waste of time.

Spending Time

As with creativity, the most common situation for *spending time* is an employer-employee relationship. In this case, money is simply a reward in exchange for the time given by the employee to the employer in the office or on the factory floor—the employer gives the employee a paycheck. The amount paid depends on the skills and productivity of the employee.

The same principle is also valid for different professional categories, what we normally call "self-employed" — consultants, attorneys, physicians, dentists, accountants. These are people who have invested their time to acquire knowledge, develop skills, and get necessary certifications so they can charge money for making their time and knowledge available to others.

As long as we agree that there is a correlation between time and money, we need to understand the exact relationship between these two resources. People will value time and money differently, depending on their current position. Some people have plenty of money but their time is limited, while others have very little money but more time. Not only that, but as life goes in seasons of abundance and scarcity, we have experienced that our perception of money and time varies from one season to another. There are instances when saving a few dollars means much more than saving time. For instance, you can buy a bag of ready-shredded salad and use it right away, or if you want to save $2, you can buy raw lettuce and spend three minutes at the kitchen counter chopping it. It's simple math: $2 saved for three minutes of work means an hourly pay (net, after taxes!) of $40—a figure that you would consider an excellent rate! Washing the car can be another similar example. What do you prefer? To spend $8 on a car wash at the gas station or spend thirty minutes in the driveway to wash it yourself? Your choice depends, of course, on what it is more important to you at the given moment. And, just for clarification, there is nothing wrong in buying shredded salad or washing the car at the gas station. But you have to be aware that the amount you are paying extra is the price of convenience; in other words, you are paying somebody for doing something you could have done yourself.

The real question is what you do with the time you save after you have paid for these services. If you choose the convenient solution and then you waste the time, it's a double waste. And this is even more important when saving every single dollar that can be saved is important—for instance, a certain period of time after you have made the decision to pay off all of your debt.

Investing Time

Investing time into certain activities will generate a constant flow of benefits. Let's explore what it means to invest time.

Investing time means to concentrate on activities with purpose and meaning. If there is no purpose or meaning in the things we do, we will waste our time. In other words, every time we do something without a purpose or meaning, that time is wasted. Every day of your existence should be counted for some kind of benefit in one or another area. This does not necessarily have to be for your own personal benefit, but a lot can be done for your family, friends, charities, or communities.

Except for Methuselah, commonly referred to as the human who lived the longest life, 969 years, nobody is remembered for longevity. Only a person's contribution to life ensures a place in history; the people we pay tribute to today are recognized for their legacy. (By the way, the Bible doesn't mention anything else noticeable about Methuselah except that he was Noah's grandfather.) Around 20,000 people visit the Sistine Chapel every single day to admire the paintings of Michelangelo Buonarroti, and millions enjoy the music created by Wolfgang Amadeus Mozart. Both of them are considered among the greatest artists in history; still, few people are aware that Michelangelo lived 89 years and Mozart only 35. They are remembered for their contributions, not for the length of their lives. The way you are using your *time*, the *purpose* and *meaning* of your daily activities today, will determine how your life is going to be in five, ten, or fifteen years from now.

Investing time means to develop a clear vision for your life. If the purpose of our life is about why we are here on this planet, a vision is a clear picture of what we want to achieve in order to fulfill that purpose. The more visual and specific we are in describing that vision, the better chance we have to bring it to reality. In other words, your commitment to make something happen in real life becomes stronger when you put on paper what you want to accomplish. The vision has to be specific, because there should be no doubt about what you want to achieve. Generic desires, such as "I'd like to make more money" or "I wish my life were better" do not qualify as vision statements. You must be specific about how much more money you want to make and clarify what it means to have a better life. For one person, "a better life" may mean "a bigger house"; for another, it may mean the ability to travel and experience new cultures or to dedicate more time to causes they are passionate about. When the vision is clearly defined, it is necessary to set up a plan for what you need to do to make it happen. A vision without a *strategy* to achieve it remains just a dream.

Investing time means to do what is right in order to maintain your integrity. When I talked about wasting time, I said that it is important to establish *time limits* on things that do not align with your vision. I also mentioned that lack of focus is one of the root causes of failure; therefore, you have to stay focused and remove any distractions that come up along the way. But perhaps a time comes in your life when you decide to clarify your vision for the future and redefine the path to move ahead. Let's say you want to start your own business but are still committed to an employee position. Your vision is clear, but your employer expects you to finalize the projects you initiated in your current position. That now feels like a distraction. You are in a situation that requires a certain amount of transitional time. While it may be tempting to immediately leave your employment or contract to jump into your own venture, doing so without fulfilling the existing commitments would be unprofessional and irresponsible. This might potentially negatively affect your professional and personal reputation. One of the greatest personal assets is *integrity*, and completing all previous commitments in a responsible manner will prove that you are a person of integrity. The way you exit your relationship with your current employer or contract partners will determine the way you enter into the process of developing your own vision. In most cases, it is necessary to have a detailed plan for transition or step down while the new vision is established. Such a plan has to clearly define those activities that do not align with your vision; as they become less important, you do not have to treat them as emergencies anymore, and you should establish how much time you will be spending on these activities.

Investing time means to help others develop themselves. This notion is very much related to the vision, the concept described in the previous section. Translating our vision into reality requires a tremendous amount of effort, and we are not able to do everything by ourselves. Bigger visions require bigger organizations, and this means human resources. A strong misconception exists among many managers today—the belief that there's no point in developing people because, when they have advanced their skills, they will leave anyway. While this may indeed sometimes happen, this belief shows only the limitations of the manager.

There is a huge difference between a manager and a true leader. While a manager is *managing resources* (including human resources) and is looking for followers, a true leader will *create leaders*. In other words, a manager will put a limitation on his followers' development, a limitation generated by the manager's lack of desire to grow himself. On the other hand, a true leader will constantly look for ways to develop his own skills and look for ways to expand his vision. His security is given by passion and drive to implement the vision, and this will attract and sustain people to his vision. While the leader is focusing on moving toward the vision and growing himself, there is a need for help, and the best help comes from people who want to grow. This is why a true leader takes the time to invest in people without any concern about their leaving the organization. Mainly due to understanding and appreciating the desire to self-develop, he will never get mad if somebody says, "It's time for me to move ahead."

Investing time means to take periodic inventories for evaluation. Once we have established a vision for our life, we should take an inventory every now and then and ask ourselves: "Did I accomplish what I said I would accomplish in the beginning of the year? Where am I in regard to what I said that I was going to accomplish? Did I stay on course? If I am off course, what took me off course? How did it hinder me?" It is important to ask yourself these questions because, if you don't, you will repeat the things of the past. If there is no adjustment, change, or transformation, things will just happen as they have always happened. If your life is the same year after year, it is a sign that you have not progressed at all. If you have the same New Year's resolutions for five years in a row, only to break them by mid-January and feel guilty for the rest of the year, it is an indication that your life has little chance for advancement.

Investing time means to prepare for each single day. "Preparation time is never wasted time" or "It's easier to catch up than to clean up." These are just two statements we hear in different contexts. In project management, the planning part is considered the most important part of a project, because planning a project well saves a lot of time during its execution. If you are like most people, life is like a race to you—you jump out of bed and into the shower, grab some food and a coffee on the run to the car, get frustrated in traffic, and keep running the whole rest of day. If you are like most people, you do not take the time to prepare for the day. You want to brutalize the alarm clock when it rings in the morning and have a very tough time getting up early. You convince yourself that the ten-minute snooze and the extra vegetative time will give you more energy, forgetting that you are tired because you watched a two-hour talk show the night before that kept you awake until midnight.

Your entire life is nothing more than a collection of days, lived one by one. It is never wasted time to take some minutes every morning getting ready in a quiet setting and thinking about the things you want to achieve during that day. You can meditate about how to accomplish them and, maybe even more important, how to react if something goes wrong. This time is well worth investing, because being more focused and prepared for the unexpected will make your day go more smoothly.

Investing time means learning something that helps you to advance in life. We live in the Information Age—everything we need to know is just a few keystrokes or mouse clicks away. More than that, we are bombarded with information. Every time we search for a certain word on the Internet, the search engines register our interest and start displaying ads and banners about that particular item or topic. Nowadays, because there is too much of it, information is something we seem to be forced to avoid rather than to look for. This confirms that everything you need to know to advance your life is here, readily available. But this is not only about *availability*. Every time you hear or read something that is supposed to make your life better, you become responsible for *doing something with it*. Passivity and choosing to remain ignorant will only hinder your growth and minimize the positive changes needed to advance your life. Of the plethora of information available, you need to discern and select those things that can be used for your benefit and growth.

But learning is much more than hearing or reading. You hear success stories or read good books, and it's not always easy to see the immediate applicability of those concepts for your life. Learning is more about *discovering*—not always a straightforward process. If a person's success is outside of your industry or main area of occupancy, you may wrongly conclude that their story is irrelevant or not applicable to you. *Investing time* means to go to the depths of the concepts so you can discover if and how it's possible to apply the same principles to your own circumstances and challenges. A direct attempt to apply other people's formulas for success without any deeper analysis and thinking will just lead to frustration and failure.

In this era of constant gratification, we are tempted to look for quick fixes to our problems. For any challenge we face, there seems to be out there a "How to Do X in Ten Easy Steps" magic formula—something that we can apply exactly as it was described and see it working. But life is much more complex than that. Like anybody else, you have your favorites among artists and athletes—

certain people you love and admire. But you have to understand that the athletes you watch now did not simply appear on the field from nowhere. They discovered their talents in their early childhood and then they worked hard to build their skills. The great artistic performance is the fruit of thousands of hours of practice. These people did not do their first rehearsal two days ago. If there is something that you do not have right now, it is not because destiny was unfair to you, but mostly because *you were unwilling to take the time to invest in your own advancement.*

Investing time means to prepare for opportunities. To a certain degree, we all live by a form of *faith*—we believe that our life will go on, we believe that some good things will happen to us, we believe that we are able to do the things we plan to do. There is nothing wrong in believing and having expectations; in fact, it is very good. The question is, how much do you prepare yourself for the good things to happen? In other words, how much time do you dedicate to positioning yourself so you are able to act and *grab opportunities* that occur? Because I will analyze opportunities in a following chapter, I will just conclude for now that time and opportunities are two of the greatest commodities we have in life. Unfortunately, these are the ones that we frequently and most often abuse. If you just believe and expect that good things will happen but you do not invest time preparing for them, it is not a true belief—just *hope*. Belief requires action before manifestation, meaning that when you believe that an opportunity will show up, you make all of the necessary preparations, including positioning yourself to be able to grab it.

Investing time means to be aware of the unexpected. We also know that sometimes unfortunate or bad things happen, and there is no guarantee that we on this planet will be spared from problems and difficulties. The question is, how much do we prepare for the unexpected? By definition, a crisis is a negative event that occurs against your will and beyond your control. Nobody is spared from crises. Positive thinking is good. And as much as you speak out and expect the things that you desire to manifest, it is very important to always take time to build a buffer for seasons when unexpected negative events occur, something I elaborated on when I talked about savings. And this is not only pertaining to finances. Of course, having a buffer of savings that can take you through difficult financial periods is very important. But equally important, this is also about building a strong emotional, psychological, and knowledge foundation. After all, it is not the crisis itself that takes you down, but the fact that you do not have the knowledge, strength, or resources to react to it in the most efficient and effective manner.

Taking the time to build such a foundation will protect you from being vulnerable. In addition, it seems like a universal paradox that the more you prepare for the unexpected, the fewer are the chances for the unexpected to occur. Even if the circumstance is of such magnitude that you are seriously harmed, being prepared enables you to limit the damages and to recover much more quickly.

Investing time means to plan for the future. We give too much importance to the unknown, and we do not plan for the future, because we believe that the future is far away and because we do not believe that we are able to influence it. It is easy to forget that our life is a collection of days and that the life we live today is the result of previous decisions. Therefore, the life of tomorrow is always influenced by the decisions made today. One of Martin Luther's most famous quotes is "Even if I knew that tomorrow the world would go to pieces, I would still plant my apple tree."

Planning for the future is a lifestyle, and therefore you have to put your time into those areas that bring advancement in your life. Planning for the future is in itself a major topic, and there are thousands of books and articles about vision, purpose, goals, and strategy that give valuable insight into this matter. A simple rule of life you can observe is that people who achieved success also planned for their success. They know that if there is no active plan to succeed, the default plan is to fail, because it's inevitable; something out of their control is going to happen. Living life with a "whatever may be, may be" attitude should never be an option for you. If you do not plan for your future, your future will not plan for you. After all, as Abraham Lincoln once said, "The best way to predict the future is to create it."

Investing time means to develop healthy relationships. We have all heard the old saying "It doesn't matter how much you know, but *who* you know." And, in many circumstances, this may apply. Great relationships make a huge difference. The best way to grow is to stay around people who know, and have achieved, more than you. These people will expose your own ignorance in some areas of life, and you will be able to work on your own self-development. You should not feel intimidated, but rather take what they have to say and internalize it, make it your own. The concept of healthy relationships is generally applicable—not only in business, but also family and social relationships. We are all part of a community and social environment, and our entire life experience improves when we dedicate time to develop our relationships.

The strength of a relationship is defined by its quality. And quality dictates that both parties must add value to each other. Being self-centered and thinking all the time "what is in it for me?" will definitely not help you building good relationships. A healthy relationship, where you make it about the other, will provide huge returns in terms of new opportunities and available resources. But these returns are the consequences of a well-groomed relationship, never goals in themselves.

Developing a relationship is like growing a fruit tree. A gardener never focuses on pulling off the fruits at the end of the branches. Instead, he focuses on taking the time to ensure the tree has its right environment: it has adequate water and the roots have air; it is free of weeds and nonproductive branches and protected from predators. So his part is to prepare and position the tree for producing the best possible fruits and let the fruits come out by themselves. This will allow the gardener to reap the best harvest. This is exactly the strategy you need to apply if you want to develop a healthy relationship, which is the outcome, an effect, of the invested quality time.

One of the most fruitful investments you can make is to develop a close relationship with a good mentor—somebody who is not just an adviser, but also a coach and role model. There are many successful businesspeople out there willing to take that responsibility and share their guidance, experience, and wisdom. But you have to understand that these people value *their time*, and they know what they can offer. Therefore, they expect from their apprentices full commitment and earnestness.

If you want to start your own business, preparing for it is invested time. Being a business owner is one of the most obvious ways to create wealth. Many people struggle with this dilemma: "Should I quit my job and start my own business?" As there is no universal right or wrong answer, I will try to highlight some main points that will, hopefully, bring some clarity. As this may be the only way in some cases, jumping directly from an employee position into a business may be a mistake, because people do not understand the real-life difficulties in owning and managing a business. There are some differences, and I will list them below.

Being an employee means a paycheck is coming constantly— whether weekly or monthly, it is an amount that keeps coming in. Being an employee means also that you can put down your job at the end of the day. Whatever you go through during the day, especially the bad experiences, you can drop the moment you leave the door. You are free to think about your other responsibilities and projects. Making sure that there is enough work for everybody in the company is not your responsibility. Tired of their boring jobs, many people are tempted to quit and take their savings (maybe even borrowing some money from their IRA or 401K accounts) in order to start a full-time business. In most cases, this ends up in failure because there is not enough capital and knowledge involved.

A business owner lives out of the profit of the business—which is what is left after everything else has been paid. It is easy to look at other people who own businesses and make money, but it may be as easy to ignore the fact that it takes time until the business reaches a level of profitability that provides a comfortable income for the owner. One of the toughest positions you can be in as a business owner is where operational revenues do not generate enough profit, so you end up making a decision whether you sustain the business or feed yourself. It is like a farmer who harvests a poor crop in a bad year—should he keep the grains for sowing, ensuring next year's crop, or should he rather take it home to feed his family?

Most businesses operate with a cost structure based on some fixed and some variable costs. The fixed costs are the ones that have to be paid regardless of revenue level. For instance, in a restaurant operation, fixed costs are related to rent, utilities, and a minimal employee structure (manager, chef, prep chef, and waiters). For the restaurant owner, this means that even before the first cup of coffee is served, these fixed costs, which may be some hundreds or even thousands of dollars every day, have already been incurred. Further, this also means that there is a breakeven level, where the restaurant balances the revenues and costs.

This is valid not only for restaurants and coffee shops; the same structure applies for many types of businesses—be it in manufacturing, trade, or service. All these parameters (cost structure, fixed costs, breakeven) are very important and should be carefully evaluated and understood before deciding to start a business. Unfortunately, one of the causes for the high failure rate in business start-ups is the lack of sustainability. People do not have enough resources to sustain the business in the early phases, which may mean some years of operational losses.

As owner of the business, you constantly think about the next day, next week, month, or even some years in advance. Everybody in the company expects you to keep them busy. Even if employees are empowered, you are the one who has to make sure they have the right framework for operations. When you leave the office, you constantly think about orders, payroll, taxes, supplies, utilities, bills to pay, and so on.

Things may be even worse for a couple who own a business together. Business and family life become so interconnected that they definitely influence each other. A disagreement or bad event at work may affect the quality time spent at home. Or vice versa—a simple dispute on a household issue may affect important business decisions.

In addition to financial challenges, every industry has its specifics that are not always easy to discover as an outsider. Therefore, being able to sustain the business during start-up is not only about providing enough funding for operations; it is also about being able to avoid the managerial errors caused by lack of knowledge in a start-up period. For instance, if you have a specific interest in home decoration, you may think that opening your own store is a good idea. But before getting there, much has to be prepared and many details need to be addressed. What do I sell? Where do I buy it from? How do I establish my prices? How quickly do I have to turn inventory in order to reach breakeven? What will make my store different from any other similar stores? And so on . . .

One of the things that I find really surprising is the number of franchise businesses for sale that are advertised as "no previous experience necessary." While it is true that franchised businesses have a much lower failure rate than regular start-ups, few franchises give to franchisees the real business-owner experience. In most cases, the combination of complex franchise agreements, stringent rules, and high royalties turns most owners of franchised businesses into regular store managers, where the only difference is that, in this case, they are the ones taking the financial risk of opening and keeping the store in operation.

All these caveats may sound discouraging and may suggest that being an employee is a far better option than starting a business. For sure, I am advocating for discovering your own purpose in life and building your own wealth through the means of business. Everything I have described here is definitely *not* meant to discourage, but rather to highlight some of the challenges and difficulties you have to take into consideration before you start the journey. The more you are aware of potential pitfalls and common mistakes, the better prepared you will be to overcome them.

The best advice would be to take the time to learn as much as possible about a business before investing in it. In addition to getting as much information as possible (books, specialized magazines and websites, industry and professional associations, seminars, fairs), practical involvement makes a huge difference, and there are several ways to do it. You can take an apprentice role with someone who has extensive experience in the business or industry and get involved in all details of the business. Or, if possible, take part-time or short-term jobs going through different positions related to the business you want to operate in. In this way, you learn without having the pressure of managing a business and generating revenues to cover fixed costs. And, maybe even more important, you avoid making costly mistakes that you end up paying for.

Another very useful way to learn without putting too much risk into a new venture is to find a way to grow the business gradually. For instance, instead of taking on a huge amount of debt by buying or opening a restaurant, you can start a concession booth at events or a small food cart business. The investment is much smaller and you can make it a profitable business without incurring many fixed costs. This is a good time to learn about food handling requirements and regulations, and it will give you important insights regarding customers' tastes and preferences.

If you would like to open a retail store, you may try first to sell some goods online. You can get your web page up in a matter of weeks (or even days) using an appropriate template that does not require much technology skill and start selling some products from your garage. As the business increases and you accumulate both knowledge and profits, you can reinvest that profit into growing the business. One of the common mistakes for many people is that after they make some thousands of dollars in profits, they rush into spending them—they buy some new appliances or maybe go on a dream vacation. In fact, those profits should be seen as growth funds that will allow taking the business to the next level, and they should be used for that purpose. Then, when the business gradually evolves to a level where profitability allows the owner to take some profits out of the business without affecting the current operations, a decision can be made whether it is time to quit a job and fully dedicate to the business. Sometimes, developing a business and taking it to the next level requires a quantum leap—which may be a significant investment needing a bank loan. But you will be much better positioned to take that loan if you have a strong foundation of experience and profitable operation at a lower level.

Chapter 8
Knowledge

"Knowledge is power" is an old aphorism that we learned in school, and the truth is that the more knowledge we possess, the easier it is for us to deal with the issues of life. In this chapter I will delve deeper into the area of knowledge, analyzing three distinct levels—*information*, *knowledge*, and *wisdom*. But first, it is essential that we understand lack of knowledge and the dangers associated with it.

Ignorance

Lack of knowledge, also known as *ignorance*, is a concept that is commonly misunderstood. Many people mistake ignorance for *stupidity*. While being stupid is lacking the ability to learn and understand, being ignorant is lacking knowledge. In other words, being stupid is something you cannot do much about. (Just to be fair, it's worth mentioning that a person with a lower IQ and lots of common sense will achieve much more in life than a person with a very high IQ and no common sense). On the other hand, being ignorant is a *choice*. We are ignorant not because we lack the ability to learn or understand, but because we *refuse* to do it. It is such a tragedy to see so many gifted and intelligent people living in ignorance simply because they refuse, for different reasons, to go through the process of learning and understanding.

I once asked myself the following question: "Would a perfect society consider a person's choice to remain ignorant to be a criminal act or a fundamental human right?" I may have an opinion about what the right answer is, but I will let others make up their own mind about it. Daymond John, the successful fashion entrepreneur and *Shark Tank* investor, said in one of his mentoring programs, "The only thing more expensive than education is ignorance" (*www.daymondjohnacademy.com*).

Why is that? There are several reasons. **First**, and what I believe is the most important, is that *ignorance makes you vulnerable to manipulation and deception.* Sometimes you can be easily influenced by people who speak out of their own ignorance, also known as "the blind leading the blind." When you are unprotected due to your lack of knowledge, you end up in a compromising or a dangerous situation that leads you into a ditch.

Much worse, when you lack knowledge, you leave yourself vulnerable to be used and misused. Essentially, you open a gateway for deception that people can use to take advantage of you and promote their own agenda. Often, simple things are purposefully presented in a complex manner to discourage you from taking the time to understand the consequences of what you are doing or agreeing to. A prime example is when you are faced with reading a lengthy, complex document or contract that contains "fine print" with a lot of legal mumbo jumbo that doesn't make any sense to you. Countless people have signed bank loans or contracts without understanding the bank-imposed limitations stated in those small print passages. Instead of reading and rereading the fine print to get a better understanding, you skip over it and sign on the dotted line without knowing exactly what you agreed to.

Deception can also captivate and misguide you to the point where you follow the wrong cause, all because you do not have the most accurate information or the knowledge required to make the best decision. You will be given erroneous information and told stories, all to take advantage of your ignorance. Ultimately, you end up believing these stories because you do not have enough knowledge to write your own.

Second, *ignorance can keep you away from something that is closer than you think.* Pretty often, you are closer than you think to what you want in life—the only thing needed is an adjustment, such as your perception about certain things. Ignorance will make you reject incoming information that is inconsistent with what you believe. It's critical to take a moment to make a careful analysis of the information and the situation you are faced with. Making a slight, yet necessary, adjustment or rethinking a few of your beliefs may lead you to the doorstep of your pursuits.

Many of us were told in school that we weren't good for anything, that we were useless and would never make it in life. Worse than that, some of our parents or loved ones may have verbally or emotionally abused us, degraded us, and never once made us feel valuable. If this is your case, some of those memories are so rooted in your mind that when someone else is encouraging you and telling you the opposite, you have a hard time believing it.

Third, *ignorance will cause you to refuse valuable advice from people you look down on.* In the process of our growing and developing as human beings, we come under the influence of the patterns and prejudices of our family and society; these influences can be exceedingly strong, so much so that they may affect our thinking to the point where we knowingly or unknowingly discredit and ignore the valuable advice of those who we believe are not at our level (socially, economically, financially). For some specific reason, whether it be ethnicity, native country, lack of formal education, or a lower social position, we simply refuse to believe that there's something to be learned from these people. What a tragic mistake! When you display your arrogant attitude of superiority, you forget that common sense and *wisdom* are available to anyone. Let's be honest: you have more to learn from someone with a simple and straightforward way of thinking than from an intellectualized idiot whose thinking is trapped in complex rationalities and philosophies.

Fourth, *ignorance will make you try in vain.* Attempting to do something without knowledge will significantly reduce your chances of success. Best-case scenario—you will succeed, but perhaps only because of a coincidence of positive circumstances. The right information and knowledge will increase your chances of success.

One of the most dangerous combinations in human behavior is *ignorance* plus *zeal*. This happens when people become excited about something they do not really understand. Working and pushing hard in an area where there is no knowledge will create much more damage than good. Zealous ignorance is like being able to move mountains but having no clue where to put them. Now that we understand how dangerous a lack of knowledge is, we can look closer at the three levels of knowing: *information, knowledge*, and *wisdom*.

Information

We live in the Information Age, and for Generation Y (aka the Millennial Generation), it is impossible to imagine a world where the only sources of information are books, newspapers and magazines, and radio and TV. The entire school system used to be based on a lecture model, where the teacher provided the information and students learned and reproduced it. Education was based on the idea that one accumulates information over the course of some years and uses the same information for the rest of one's professional life. Well, times have changed significantly since the development of computers and the Internet. Information has suddenly become available (although not always free of charge), and the amount of available information is exploding. According to statistics, the Internet has accelerated the process of accumulating information. In the first years, when the Internet was still a novelty, the amount of available information doubled in the six years between 1993 and 2000. Since then, the time it takes for the amount of information to double has constantly decreased. At the moment of writing this book, in 2015, the amount of available information on the Internet doubles *every 35 days*.

Yahoo was one of the first companies offering free e-mail services. In 2000, those free Yahoo mailboxes had a limit of . . . 4 MB. No, that is not a typo. At that time, four megabytes were enough for most people because that capacity allowed them to store hundreds of plain-text e-mails. Such a figure seems ridiculous today, notably when a single attached file can exceed many times that size. As technology continues to develop at this accelerated pace, the problem we face today is rather the opposite—there is *too much* information, and it seems more and more difficult to find the *relevant* information.

But the good news is that everything you need to know is available for you just a couple of keystrokes and mouse clicks away. You are sure to find useful information for whatever you want to do— information that shows you what and how things need to be done.

If you plan a trip to a faraway destination, you can sit at home in the comfort of your living room and find out how to get there, where you can stay, and how much you have to pay for travel, meals, and lodging. You can read opinions from people who have been there and learn about their experiences. So if you travel somewhere and you missed something worth visiting or if you have been cheated somehow during your journey, you do not have much of an excuse because, in most cases, everything you needed to know was somewhere on the Internet. When taking on the challenges of DIY projects at home (fixing, remodeling, decorating), you make it your purpose to find information about how to complete the project. Also, most of the big-name hardware stores put a lot of effort into providing practical advice on how to use products you buy, hence more information. When organizing a special event or home party, you can find out whatever you need to know to make it successful: what to cook and how to cook it, how to decorate the room and the tables, fun activities for you and your guests.

A lot of information is free—you find it on the Internet. Some information you do have to pay for—like conferences, seminars, and other resources. And more importantly, you have to be aware that *really valuable information* is never free—you need to be willing to make an effort to get it. But one way or another, the information is available to you, so you cannot say, "Oh, I wish I had known that."

Essential to your development is the commitment to regularly increase your level of information; if you do not have this commitment, it will limit your growth. *No one can rise above the level of the information he or she possesses.* While you already possess a certain amount of information about nearly everything, that is still not enough. Most definitely, you can carry out some activities and tasks with your current store of information, but this is valid only at a basic level. Complicated tasks require moving to the next level, which is . . . *knowledge.*

Knowledge

If information were enough to carry out all activities, the notion of education would be unnecessary. We would simply search the web or open a couple of books and start doing whatever we have to do. But indeed, it's much more than that. Possessing the information alone will not equip us to perform a task at a professional level.

Imagine a kid who dreams of becoming a successful surgeon. He sees himself in the emergency room, performing the most complicated surgeries. For some reason, he ends up on another professional path, but somewhere deep inside him is still the desire and passion to perform surgeries. All the *information* needed is available to him—the best surgery books, human body encyclopedias, DVDs, and any kind of specialized literature. He has access to all of it, yet if he were to try to fulfill his youthful dream and perform a surgery, it would probably end in disaster. He needs to be educated and trained about how to *use* that information.

We can find many other examples where the *availability* of information will not enable us to become proficient in our industry. Information is useful and it has its place, but information alone is not enough; we need to move from information to the level of *knowledge*—that is, *the ability to use and apply information* in a meaningful way and deliver results according to our own and others' expectations. In other words, knowledge is about *accumulated learning*. You may have the desire and passion to do something, you may have the access to information that is needed to do it, but you must possess the skills to use and apply that information in a manner that creates an impact. Everything you learn should make or spark a change in your own or someone else's life. If it doesn't, it means that all efforts and time put into learning were wasted.

Some professional careers require a formal education, with tests and exams, because of the public and social responsibilities attached to that profession. Medical professions are in charge of people's health; this is why, when you need medical support, you look for a "good doctor." The quality of the work performed by building contractors, electricians, and plumbers has certain safety impacts; an airplane pilot carries with him the responsibility of some hundreds of people traveling in the plane, let alone the potential damages on the ground should the plane crash.

There is no value in remaining at the information level if you only retain it and not use it. With all the resources available, you can find in a couple of hours more information than you will be able to read in a lifetime. The purpose of acquiring information is to transfer and transform it into skills that can be used to change the surrounding reality. An important distinction must be made at this point: *we must understand the difference between sense knowledge and revelation knowledge*. As mentioned, knowledge is the ability to use and apply information—information that we receive from different external sources. Depending on how much we internalize this information into our mind and behavior, we will operate either in *sense* knowledge or *revelation* knowledge.

Sense knowledge can also be seen as a form of *mental assent*—which is agreeing with something without having any understanding why you should act upon it. When you operate in this mode, you are aware of that thing; you understand its form and you understand what triggers it. You also understand the effects or consequences. But you do not really understand the essence, the core of the thing. For instance, it is not necessary to know anything about the law of gravity. Still, you learn pretty early in life that if you hold something in your hands and release it, it will fall onto the ground. You had no understanding of why this happened, but you knew how it works. Another example is a car's engine. You know that you have to start it using the ignition key and you know that it needs fuel. If something is wrong, you have an alarm light. You don't need to know anything about the combustion process or compression rates in order to use a car.

Your entire sense knowledge is based on senses—you see, you hear, you feel—what happens, but you do not understand *why* things happen. You do not necessarily get to the core of an event. And if you do not understand why things work in the way they work, you are vulnerable to deception. This is why you need to move from information to knowledge and then, from sense knowledge to revelation knowledge.

Revelation knowledge occurs when you understand not only *what* happens around you, but also *why* things happen. It occurs when you internalize the information you have and make use of it because you understand how and why you use it. We humans are constantly developing and creating systems with increased complexity, but we fail on the basics. We managed to put a complex machine on Mars and control it from millions of miles away, but we cannot agree with our neighbors about snow shoveling the driveway. Or even worse, have fights with our spouse about how to squeeze the toothpaste—from the middle, or from the end?

Our educational system is mostly based on sense knowledge. Sense knowledge alone will not change your life. Sense knowledge is limited to what your body and your mind are able to assimilate. If your mind and your body cannot relate to the received inputs, the

191

information is rejected or misused. Although there is more knowledge available now than at any other time in history, it appears as though we have not increased our *understanding*. We are not able to come to the deep knowledge of the basics, because it seems like "the basics" is just a moving target. In a world of constant change, the basic values and fundamentals of the society are constantly redefined.

Sense knowledge is not enough to take us to the next level. When you don't have any knowledge in an area, you may believe that sense knowledge, knowing what do to, is all it takes. This is a trap, because when you get it, there is still something missing. Only revelation knowledge will be able to take you to the next level. Living beyond your existing boundaries will require faith that you can get there before you get there. Creativity and "thinking outside the box" have their roots in revelation knowledge. All inventions of mankind are based on revelation knowledge. Having deep understanding about why things work in the way they work allows you to discover new realms and take things beyond what is readily available.

One of the best-known learning models in psychology, also called the "four stages of competence," is the Conscious Competence Model. Developed by Noel Burch at Gordon Training International, this model makes a distinction between the following:

- the *unconscious competent*—a person who is competent in one area *without being aware of it*. This person is "the natural" who knows what to do and manages well in most circumstances and situations, but does not necessarily know why.

- the *conscious competent*—a person who is competent in one area and *is well aware of it*. Not only does the person manage circumstances, he is also able to explain his actions. Furthermore, she is able to transfer knowledge to others.

Remaining in sense knowledge is similar to being in the unconscious competence area. This is dangerous because it creates a mismatch between your words, thoughts, and actions. Consistency is a key ingredient of character. Your life is a life of integrity when words, thoughts, and actions align with each other and reflect your inner values. When you agree to something verbally without aligning it to your thoughts and actions, you are creating a mismatch that allows for self-deception, because you end up having information in your mind without transferring it into your real life. It is like knowing something but not being able to make it work, and this is one of the major problems in our society today.

Wisdom

Wisdom is the highest level that can be achieved in the area of knowledge. Thus far, we have discovered the importance of access to information. Better yet, we have also gained the understanding that we need learning to make that information applicable. Simply put, information has no value if we do not know what it is used for and how it should be applied. We have also learned that there are two types of knowledge—sense knowledge (where we know what to do) and revelation knowledge (when we know why we are doing it). It may be easy to mistake revelation knowledge for wisdom. But there are some other dimensions that differentiate the two.

The **first** distinction is the element of experience. According to *The Merriam-Webster Dictionary*, wisdom is *knowledge that is gained by having many experiences in life*. This means that even revelation knowledge, which is deeper than sense knowledge, needs to be taken through different experiences of life in order to provide full benefits.

Second, *wisdom* is strongly tied to *insight*. Insight is the ability to go to the core of issues and problems and discern deep causes and components. It also means having the ability to understand things that most people do not understand. Insight goes hand in hand with *complexity*. The more complex a problem is, the more insight it requires to solve it.

Third, wisdom requires a *big picture understanding*—not just how things work and why they work in the way they work, but also how they interact in a wider context. While knowledge can be very specific to a certain area, field of activity, or industry (even to the level of expertise), wisdom is much broader and provides understanding of both *facts* and *emotions* involved in a certain situation. This is why we have numerous examples of wise people leading multimillion and billion dollar companies without much formal education, while people with PhDs are just employees on the payroll. These PhD pundits are essential to the entire operation because they provide top knowledge in their area of expertise; still, they do not possess the entire big picture mentality in order to run the full operation. Therefore, their role is limited to providing as much knowledge as needed, when required.

Fourth, having wisdom means being able to judge, in a reasonable manner, circumstances and situations at hand, so one can act in order to achieve the best outcome. As there is always a most adequate solution for every circumstance or challenge, wisdom cannot be disconnected from creativity. One of the best examples of applied wisdom is the "cut the baby in half" story in the Bible. Solomon, recently appointed as King of Israel, had to judge between two women. While living in the same house, each of them had delivered a baby. One morning, one of the babies was found dead, and one of the mothers claimed, "This woman's child died in the night, because she lay upon it. And she arose at midnight, and took my son from beside me, while thine handmaid slept, and laid it in her bosom, and laid her dead child in my bosom." As the other woman denied it, King Solomon had to judge who was telling the truth. He called for a sword, stating that the only fair solution was to cut the living baby in two and give to each woman a half of the dead body. As one of the women said "Oh, my lord, give her the living child, and in no wise slay it," while the other answered "It shall be neither mine nor thine; divide it," Solomon knew who was telling the truth (1 Kings 3, 16-28). Regardless of your religious standpoint, whether you believe that things really happened this way or you think this is just a nice story, you have to admit that it is indeed a very good example of *applied wisdom*. Although young and relatively inexperienced in matters of life, Solomon had the insight and understanding to go to the core of the issue—what would make the difference between a real mother and a pretending one? Understanding that a true mother would care more about the baby than about herself, Solomon was able to judge correctly.

Fifth, *true wisdom requires a humble attitude*, admitting there is always something more to discover. Arrogance is a wisdom killer.

Moving from Information to Knowledge and Then to Wisdom

The area of knowledge, with its three levels (information, knowledge, wisdom), cannot be described using the same pattern (wasting, spending, and investing) as used for the other resources I analyzed (creativity, time, and opportunities). This is because knowledge is gained by taking information and investing time and creativity in order to learn how to apply it in the right way, which leads us to *sense knowledge*. Furthermore, we invest time to understand *why* we do the things we do, which leads us to *revelation knowledge*. And finally, we invest *time* and *creativity* to gain *experience* and *insight*, helping us to reach the *wisdom* level.

Moving from information to wisdom, through all these stages, is a step-by-step investment process, and this is a process that never stops, because wisdom is not limited; it grows permanently and perpetually. With the other resources I analyzed what it means to waste, spend, or invest; in this case we will look at the benefits of wisdom.

Benefits of Operating in Wisdom

Wisdom is more important than money. When someone has money but lacks the wisdom to manage it, he or she will eventually lose all of it. Accumulating wealth and gaining wisdom are two processes that must be developed simultaneously; otherwise there will be a mismatch that causes a quick deterioration of the wealth. This is why at least 70 percent of lottery millionaires end up losing in just a few years all the money they once had. And this is also why many people who inherit fortunes end up broke. Gaining wisdom will eventually lead to wealth regardless of the starting point. No matter how little you have to start with, making the right choices with the little you have will always lead to more.

Wisdom allows you to develop healthy relationships. We addressed the importance of developing healthy relationships in the previous chapter; I claimed that time allocated for this purpose is well-invested time. I mentioned that healthy relationships are those relationships where your own interests are waived in favor of common or even other people's interest and priorities. A good relationship represents an *investment.* No matter what type of relationship we are talking about—personal, business, or social—we are talking about two parts that together make more than each part separately.

Wisdom allows you to see beyond self-centered interests to discover the common benefits. If you see a relationship only through selfish or "what's in it for me" eyes and focus only on what you can get, you do not and will not invest any type of resources into it. As with anything else, when you do nothing but make withdrawals, you become broke or bankrupt. An important reason why wisdom allows you to relate better is that wisdom provides a better understanding of human needs. If whomever you relate to has needs, and if you understand those needs, you will be able to relate to them in a way that meets those needs.

Wisdom is a source of self-confidence and security. Insecure people are self-absorbed, thinking too much about themselves, always looking for validation, and therefore focusing on their own interests and concerns. They feel that they need to prove who they are and what they can do; this is why their focus is always wrong. On the other hand, being wise will allow you to know where you stand and what to count on in every circumstance of life. You will understand the power of wisdom and will not need to struggle to promote your own agenda in every situation. As you work on creating win-win situations in every encounter and focus on benefits of a relationship rather than your individual desires, you will avoid someone else's manipulations and attempts at deception.

Wisdom increases your self-esteem. In the same way as it helps you to build your self-confidence, wisdom helps you to increase your self-esteem. It develops your ability to find creative solutions for the problems you face—be it in personal life or professional career. In time, you are able to deal with increasingly difficult circumstances, and as this process goes on, you will be able to face your fears with increased confidence and higher self-esteem, knowing that you can overcome any situation.

Wisdom contains the essence of progress and therefore allows you to adapt to an ever-changing environment. Every step of progress in history is a result of finding a solution to a certain problem. Wisdom plays an important role in it because it provides a required *deeper understanding.* Many of the problems occur due to changing environments, and possessing wisdom gives you a better chance to adapt more rapidly to a new environment. This is even valid when changes are not predictable. Although some changes may take you by surprise, the *understanding* and *insight* will be the necessary equipment needed to react.

Wisdom allows you to avoid having bad days. As long as wisdom is also based on experiences, you can see everything that happens as a learning experience. This does not mean having a passive or "whatever may be, may be" attitude, but rather enjoying every single day of your life, regardless of what you go through. Humans have no guarantee of a trouble-free life—we all experience ups and downs. Still, assessing the facts and trying to understand what happened and why it happened allows you to learn from every situation. So every day, even those days that you would normally consider "bad days," is just an opportunity to gain *wisdom*.

Wisdom helps you to eliminate frustration. As long as you understand how things relate to each other, you are able to control your reactions. Suddenly, the things that would normally ruin your day are somewhat controllable, simply because your react differently, in a more positive manner.

Wisdom provides discernment. When I discussed ignorance, I revealed that it makes us vulnerable to manipulation and deceit. On the other hand, insight, which is a characteristic of wisdom, protects us because it provides the necessary *discernment* to easily distinguish between good and bad opinions. Deception is a deliberate misrepresentation of the truth. Sometimes it is a direct lie, but not always. In fact, most deceptions occur when people highlight only positive aspects of a matter while avoiding mention of the negative aspects.

In addition to protection, discernment will also allow you to evaluate the criticism you face. There is always a distinction between *constructive criticism* and *negativism*. People who want your best in life will always tell you what you can improve. When they reveal your weaknesses, they do it privately and provide suggestions for improvement. On the other hand, negative voices will be expressed publicly and will focus on the negative without giving any form of support. While constructive criticism is very important for your development, the envy-based negative criticism should be ignored.

Discernment will also protect you from associating with a wrong agenda. There are many good causes around that need and deserve your support, but there are also causes built on wrong reasons, desire for revenge, offense, or even lack of forgiveness. You need discernment before endorsing such a cause, because you may become guilty by association.

Wisdom makes you aware of what is to your own advantage. As ignorance makes us vulnerable to other people's manipulation, wisdom makes us aware of our advantages, leading us to an "I know more" position. This enables you to act taking advantage of your wisdom. Saying "your advantage" is not meant in a selfish way, making things about yourself. There are many circumstances when the common interests of a business, an organization, or even a community are at stake, and a leader's wisdom will ensure that decisions are made in the favor of that entity. But there are also many cases when you face strong competition for gaining a better position or privileges. It is about "eat or be eaten," and in such cases, the outcome depends on which side possesses the wisdom of playing the cards in a way that promotes his own advantage.

Wisdom gives you the possibility of always being in control. We do not always have control over circumstances around us, but we always have control over our reactions to these circumstances and how we react to what happens as a result of these circumstances. The deeper understanding gives you the possibility to always be on top of the situations you face. "Being in control" does not refer to a bossy position, but to the fact that you can control your own life. Although there will always be events outside your own control, you have to acknowledge that the ultimate responsibility for your life resides with you, and this relates to how you react to those circumstances or events.

Wisdom allows you to be ahead of the curve. "There is nothing new under the sun" is an old saying, as is "History always repeats itself." This means that few changes are indeed unpredictable, and most shifts are predictable and based on transitions; they represent patterns that can be observed and learned. Wisdom enables you to discover and understand these patterns, and while most people are taken by surprise, the wise ones can take action and be ahead of the curve. Robert Kiyosaki points out in his book *Why We Want You to Be Rich*, written together with Donald Trump, "Once you understand predictability, you will see it everywhere."

Wisdom allows you to make moves against the trends. Unfortunately, most people have a pack mentality—they need somebody to show them the way. Not because they do not have the brains to act on their own, but because they did not take the time to build up the necessary understanding that enables them to make the right decisions. Being insecure about how to handle a certain difficult situation will cause you to look for somebody to follow—it may be a strong leader or it may be the majority of the people. And history shows that the majority report is, most of the time, wrong. Wisdom will allow you to understand when it is the right time to move against the crowd. When people move in masses in one direction, there are two possibilities. If the masses are right, the benefits will be shared by a lot of people. This means minimal benefits for each of them. In this case, the few people who acted against the movement will lose. But if the masses are wrong and things move in an opposite direction, all benefits are shared by the few who had the wisdom (but also patience and guts) to bet against the crowd. All those who were in the crowd will lose. But those who bet against the crowd, because they are few, will gain a lot.

One of the best examples that illustrates this concept is the unfolding of today's precious metals market. Gold prices (per ounce) rose from $850 in January 2009 to over $1,900 in September 2011, in a time when many analysts predicted that declining confidence in the US dollar would push gold even higher. The move of silver was similar—from $11 to $43 (with a peak of $48 registered in May 2011). When the prices kept increasing, many outsiders jumped into the game. They were either motivated by greed (saw this as an opportunity to make significant gains) or panic (were afraid of losing their savings). Since September 2011, gold prices have decreased from $1,900 to around $1,250 (January 2015), and silver has decreased from $43 to below $17 per ounce.

As I pointed out when I discussed investing in precious metals, one thing to be understood is that they are priced like commodities, and the market price is not just the price of a direct exchange of physical metal vs. money. It is a result of many different operations, including futures trading (options), selling and buying of future production, and sale of leased gold by bullion banks. In other words, the market price of gold and silver is not directly a result of physical supply and demand of the metal itself, but very much involves trading expectations rather than physical metal. This makes the market extremely volatile and subject to manipulation. And this is in fact something that is claimed by analysts who specialize in precious metal markets—that the decline in prices that the market experienced throughout 2013 was the result of manipulating expectations by some players in the market—with the purpose of undermining precious metals as a safe haven and a money standard.

At the current time, there are two opinions. One states that precious metals have gone through a bubble and the higher prices will never come back. The prices are low and will remain low because the interest in storing precious metals is limited (central bank reserves, jewelry, and technology). The other opinion claims that, throughout history, precious metals have always absorbed, through higher prices, the excessive supply of fiat currency.

Without understanding the way this market operates, it is very hard to formulate an opinion. For a person who bought gold at $1,900 and silver at $43, expecting further increases, the decline to $1,200 for gold and $20 for silver represents a disaster. The question is, what will this person do? Most probably, the majority of the people who bought at peak and experienced the decline already sold their gold and silver. They simply accepted the loss and they will hardly ever get involved in precious metals again. They believed the first opinion—that gold and silver prices will remain low.

On the other hand, some other people, and they are clearly in a minority, saw the decline as an opportunity to buy more silver and gold. Although they may have bought at peak, they are not discouraged. They believe the second opinion—that precious metals are *the only* store of value and they will absorb the excessive supply of fiat currency.

Only the future will tell what the right decision was. But we should remember that if the second opinion proves to be right and gold and silver prices bounce back to even higher levels, the minority who believed it will reap the benefits—because they were of the few who bought gold and silver in a time when many stayed away from it. At the same time, people who disregard gold and silver may see all their savings vanish due to inflated fiat currencies. It is only *wisdom* that provides the *understanding* that allows you to make the right judgment in these kinds of situations.

Chapter 9
Opportunities

Our entire lives are simply a collection of days, a mere sequence of moments and hours. Although we feel that our entire life lies ahead and the future is somehow far away, we should never forget that we live one day at a time. Life is consumed in real time, right now, right where we are at every single moment. Every single day is unique and open for new *opportunities*. Opportunity and time are two of the greatest commodities given to humanity, but unfortunately, these are the two commodities we abuse most often. We consistently connect the idea of opportunity with something good, something we desire. *The Merriam-Webster Dictionary* defines *opportunity* as "a favorable juncture of circumstances" or "a good chance for advancement and progress."

A person who lives a fulfilled life understands that the greatest enemy of life is not death, but regret for the loss of opportunities that could have been used to bring enjoyment and fulfillment during his life journey. Unfortunately, none of us can turn back time, but there are important questions each of us should ask ourselves once in a while, such as "When I am in my senior years and I reflect back on my life, will I be regretful of the opportunities I neglected or didn't seize?" If you fail to seize those life-changing opportunities and thereby fail to make the most of your days by neglecting to make a significant daily contribution, you will essentially be collecting one empty day after another, and ultimately you will reach the end of your life with nothing to show but empty memories . . . empty days and regrets.

Opportunities are constantly staring you in the face, which is why it is senseless for anyone to be "sitting in the grandstand of life," bored to tears and, even worse, living in poverty. You are surrounded by people who have needs—and those needs, whether big or small, represent huge opportunities. Your goal should be to find a need and meet it. *Satisfying the appetites of society will generate streams of revenues that, if properly managed, will lead to wealth.* Before analyzing the ways we waste, spend, or invest opportunities, let us review some facts.

Fact #1: Opportunities wait to be recognized. Opportunities are all around us. Still, they are not easily discovered, because they are anything but obvious. Opportunities do not knock on the door; they stand by silently waiting to be recognized. In his book *Rich Dad, Poor Dad*, Robert Kiyosaki said,

> Great opportunities are not seen with your eyes. They are seen with your mind. Most people never get wealthy simply because they are not trained financially to recognize opportunities in front of them (p. 125).

Although not too recent, one of the best examples of opportunity to be recognized is the development of the Swiss watch industry throughout the centuries. During the Middle Ages, church leaders prohibited use of jewelry by the monks, as this was considered a sign of pride. That was probably bad news for jewelers, but not for some watchmakers, who saw the entire situation as a golden opportunity: to decorate their watches. After all, everybody needed a watch—including monks, who had the chance to show off without breaking the rules. Thus, an entire industry was born.

Fact #2: Opportunities go unnoticed because they may look like an unfair change. We tend to be more preoccupied with the package than its content, and we are tempted to look for value only if the package glitters. We seem to agree that "not everything that glitters is gold," but the truth is that we are not inclined to look for valuable content that is wrapped in a plain, unassuming package.

You may still believe that a great opportunity is something that comes out of the blue, served on a silver tray, and made ready for your indulgence and enjoyment. What you miss is the fact that an opportunity is rarely ever beautifully packaged; it usually comes in a plain brown wrapper, that is, "working clothes." Furthermore, when you are faced with paying the price of hard work, you think that you might be robbed, or it is an unfair exchange. You fail to see this effort as a *golden opportunity*, and you reject it because you focus on the grime and debris that needs removing in order to reveal the treasure inside. No diamond will ever shine in its natural state. Its beauty can be discovered only by those who search for it, dig it out, and polish it into perfection—in other words, only people who put in the time and effort to reveal true value will reap the rewards of that value.

Sometimes great opportunities can be hidden behind disappointments. The negative outcome of a situation or a human interaction may be just the right element needed to trigger a revelation, a discovery, or a new idea. In a setback situation, your focus should be on how to turn it around for the better rather than focusing on the negative, victimizing yourself and finding excuses.

Fact #3: Opportunities are circumstances where abilities are manifested. As I noted when I talked about creativity, the echoing voices saying "there is nothing good in me" are absolutely, without a doubt, false! Everybody has a set of abilities, strengths, gifts, and talents. In many of us, they still lie dormant or undiscovered, but the truth is that there is something valuable in each person. An opportunity is a circumstance where you can bring inner abilities into manifestation. Let's be clear that this is not about education. Education is good and important, but education will simply enhance what a person already has on the inside. Education alone does not create abilities; it helps you to transform abilities into skills and thus make efficient use of the already existing inner abilities.

Fact #4: Seizing opportunities makes winners. Winners are always in the minority, not the majority. In life, few people really win. Both winners and losers have the same opportunities when facing the same circumstances. One of the main differences between winners and quitters is that winners are always aware of their surroundings and the tasks at hand. Winners stay engaged, while quitters are, in most cases, too self-absorbed to recognize an opportunity when it presents itself. The way we react in the midst of circumstances, whether they are favorable or not, will determine whether we will *grasp an opportunity* or let it go, making us a winner or not.

Fact #5: Grasping an opportunity is not a short-term action. Truly acting on an opportunity is backed by a long time perspective, work, and commitment. Getting started is easy, but the challenge is in persevering when developments turn unfavorable and the temptation to quit rears its ugly head. These moments, when you feel like quitting, become "life-defining moments"—moments that make or break your success. It's in these moments when it's crucial to gather all resources, including mental and psychological, to assist in sustaining you and making sure you keep moving. This may be hard to do, especially in the initial phases of a venture, because it seems there is no or very little progress in your endeavors. It's comparable to building a foundation, where all the critical and most important work is underground and not visible. But you must keep your focus, with a clear understanding that whatever you are building requires a strong foundation. The stronger the foundation, the more weight it can bear.

Linus Torvalds, the creator of Linux, the operating system that powers most Internet servers and 96 percent of the world's supercomputers, said in an interview for the Computer History Museum documentary *The Origins of Linux*, "When you do not have anything to start with, you do not even see that you are making any progress . . . You are going one instruction at a time basically. But then, when you get pass a certain phase, things actually start moving much faster." (*www.youtube.com/watch?v=WVTWCPoUt8w*)

Fact #6: Opportunities come in areas where new value is created. Our subconscious mind is a clearinghouse for our actions. Great ideas enter our mind, where they are evaluated. Some we act upon; others we abort. Your main challenge is to get rid of older, nonproductive ideas to make room for new ones. As a rule, it is easier to learn something new than to remove old thinking.

The main key in turning an opportunity *idea* into a *solution* is *creating value*. A problem is something that consumes unnecessary resources. The solution will eliminate this problem's use of resources and, therefore, will be perceived as valuable. Most of the world's problems today are problems with really open-ended solutions. As a result, in her seminars about entrepreneurship, Tina Seelig, the executive director of Stanford Technology Ventures Program, is actively inspiring students to become more and more comfortable solving problems. In fact, she would even encourage them to go out looking for problems. Our daily circumstances provide dozens of problems that everybody faces, yet only a small percentage of us think about turning them into opportunities. The bigger the problem, the bigger the opportunity. There is no reason for anyone to say, "I don't have any money in my pocket" because, by observing our surroundings, it becomes obvious that there are always opportunities to create value. Now that we have a better understanding of opportunities, let us see what it means to *waste* and *invest* opportunities.

Wasting Opportunities

You waste opportunities when you procrastinate. As a reminder, *time* and *opportunities* are two of the most misused resources we have in life. Procrastination might be the number one reason for missed opportunities. When we procrastinate, we ignore an open window of opportunity to advance our life. If we keep ignoring one window of opportunity after another, we will eventually end up in poverty. There are many reasons why you may procrastinate. Sometimes, you are simply lazy. (Sorry, no offense—this happens to everybody.) Other times, you are unsure of the outcome, and thus you hesitate initiating an action. Or perhaps you feel that the timing is not right. Another reason you procrastinate is that you feel that you have to finish other projects or commitments you started earlier or that you should be better prepared and learn more about what you are getting into.

All these reasons may be considered "legitimate" ones for not acting immediately, but regardless of the reason, procrastination is nothing but a form of deception. When you agree to postpone "just a little bit," that "little bit" turns into days, months, and years until it is too late and the window of opportunity is simply not there anymore.

You waste opportunities when they seem too good to be true. Similar to what sometimes happens with our own creativity, in that we reject some of our own ideas because they seem too good to be true, it is likewise with opportunities: we tend to protect ourselves from other people's deceit and consequently we reject the idea that we may actually be faced with a good opportunity. This is a moment when *wisdom* and *discernment* play important roles. Before moving ahead, you must look beyond the surface and try to discover first the *need* that lies behind the opportunity and determine if this need, that has yet to be exploited, can be satisfied by *creating value.*

You waste an opportunity when it's so simple that you think somebody must have thought of it before. This again aligns with the notion of wasted creativity. Opportunities are discovered when we encounter difficult situations that require a solution. Many examples can be given, but one of the best known is the Post-it. Used today worldwide, those simple, multicolored, semi-sticky labels were invented by Arthur Fry, a young engineer who, while practicing in his church choir, had a problem keeping in order the bookmarks used during rehearsals. As the songbooks were opened and closed so often, the bookmarks had a tendency to fall out. Creating a partly glued note was the ideal solution; the glue was strong enough to make it adhere to the pages, but weak enough to be removed without damaging the paper.

When finding this kind of simple solution, it is quite normal to think, "Oh, no . . . it is *too* simple. Somebody must have thought about this already, and if it is not out there in the market, it means this doesn't work." People having great, yet simple, ideas do not see themselves as being the ones called to solve that problem, while in fact, the solution is available to anybody, on a "first come-first served" basis.

You waste opportunities when you lack the motivation to press through obstacles. Every great endeavor is eventually met by some type of barrier; a challenge will present itself or something will go wrong. We have no guarantee that things will go smoothly from the beginning to the end. In fact, history shows that resistance is much stronger when an opportunity creates a radical change. The more radical the change, the stronger the resistance we will face. This is why, when you meet an obstacle, you are supposed to keep thinking about the destination (i.e., keep your eyes on the prize) and find ways to go around, over, or through it, even if it takes more time or requires more resources to reach the goal. Furthermore, after you have dealt with one barrier and are back on the right track, you may meet another one. This is not a sign that you should give up, but rather that you should dig deeper and find the necessary motivation to proceed and overcome this barrier as well. Regardless of how many obstacles you meet, it is vital that you continue until you get to the place you want to be.

If you quit before reaching the destination, it means that you *wasted* that opportunity. Robert Herjavec, the founder of the Herjavec Group and *Shark Tank* investor, said in one of his interviews, "You have to get to the point where the pain of not achieving your goals is greater than the pleasure of achieving your goals. Pain is the greatest motivator when you are stuck" (*www.youtube.com/watch?v=ThxtgKN2cU8*).

You waste opportunities when your pride gets in the way. It happens once in a while that we are asked to be involved in different ventures that may seem to us too basic, trivial, or below our social status. It may be a community project, a charity, or even some paid work, but because of pride, we feel that we are too special to get involved in an activity that is "below our level." If this happens to you, and your pride hinders you from getting involved, you may miss some big opportunities. Why do I say that? First of all, such projects may offer the chance to be part of something bigger than yourself, and by choosing to stay out, you are depriving yourself of the feeling of being a giver or contributor, a feeling that is so important for building your self-esteem and your self-worth (please do not forget that there is a difference between self-esteem and pride).

Very often we confuse significance with attention. We may be involved in an activity that is important, but we do not necessarily get much attention. The need to be significant is a legitimate human need that lies deep inside of us. A secure person will do important things that create an impact for others even if she does not get much public recognition for that. On the other hand, *need for attention* is a sign of insecurity. An insecure person will be involved in impactful activities only as long as he or she can receive some public attention. When choosing involvement, an insecure person will always prefer attention and recognition instead of importance.

Such projects are excellent opportunities to meet people and establish new contacts—people who can open new doors for you. And, equally important, you are given the chance to prove your faithfulness and dedication, even in areas "below your dignity" or where you may feel overqualified. One particular example where pride can cause you to waste opportunity is when, while looking for a job, you refuse temporary assignments that are below your qualifications. By refusing such assignments, you ignore the fact that many companies are deliberately using temporary contracts in order to identify good candidates for their open positions. If the people they temporarily employ deliver according to their criteria and expectations, they are offered permanent employment. If the performance is poor, the company will just ask for the next in line. So this would be an excellent opportunity to get your foot in the door and prove your qualities. But if your ego gets in the way and hinders you from taking such assignments, you waste it.

You waste opportunity when jealousy and envy take over. Although many people mistake jealousy for envy, these two feelings are quite different. The commonality lies in the fact that both have an evil nature—they focus on desires about someone else's possessions. The difference is that *jealousy* is wanting what someone else has, while *envy* is acknowledging that if one cannot get it, then nobody else should have it either. One particular example is when somebody states that certain athletes do not deserve to be paid multimillion-dollar salaries. This is simply hypocrisy; the person saying this would like to have the necessary gifts and talents to play in a professional league, but they don't have them. Therefore, they think, because nobody is willing to pay a dime to see them playing ball, the professional players should not be paid too much either.

Jealousy and envy are opportunity killers because they keep you focusing on what you do not have, and this will hinder your creativity and ability to discover opportunities that allow you to soar (and, of course, get what you want).

Investing in Opportunities

You invest in opportunities when you challenge the status quo. We have become accustomed to taking everything for granted and living our lives accordingly. As puppets of society, we have adapted without hesitation to its thoughts, ideas, and interests. If you think that things should remain as they have always been, your life will be empty. You are simply nothing more than a passive spectator. With all the good things happening around us, you get no credit for that. In fact, there is *always* something happening around you, and if you do not act when opportunities arise, you will miss them, and later on you will look back and have regrets. Great doors of opportunity open when you ask a simple question like "why do we have to do it this way?" or when you reject statements like "we have always done it this way" or "everybody does it the same way."

Every time you challenge the status quo and ask questions, you not only discover opportunities but also position yourself to take advantage of them. This doesn't imply that you should rebel against law and order, but you should always ask . . . *why?*

You invest in opportunities when you embrace change. This may seem related to challenging the status quo, but it is indeed different. While challenging the current state is about your direct involvement in creating a change, *embracing change* is about observing, accepting, and acting upon changes that occur around you. If you are like most people, you prefer your comfort zone and are tempted to see change as an enemy. Still, you should not fight it, but welcome it as a friend, because when it comes, it creates a pressure that forces you to adapt and consequently discover new areas. In fact, comfort is your enemy because, when you are content with what's around you, you become less effective in everything you do and you miss those opportunities provided by change.

Having said that, it is important to understand that not everything is supposed to change. There are fundamental principles of life and values that represent sound anchors in our individual lives. Named by *Newsweek* as one of the top fifty rabbis in the US (also known for his teachings about wealth and author of *Thou Shall Prosper*), Rabbi Daniel Lapin explains in his program *The Gathering Storm*,

> The more things change, the more we need to depend on the things that never change. We need to define those things that are non-negotiable in our life—spiritual, financial, marriage, family, business, and relationships. When these non-negotiables are clearly defined, it is easier to not be distracted by the surrounding noise. (*www.rabbidaniellapin.com*)

You invest in opportunities when you put passion into taking advantage of them. Seeing opportunities in every circumstance requires *passion*. When there is no passion, life becomes routine—a boring routine. Every single circumstance becomes familiar and unchallenging. Familiarity acts like a poison, like an anesthetic that takes passion out of function. It is a vicious cycle; when you lose some of your passion, you also lose the desires. When you lose the desires, you lose the motivation. When you lose your motivation, you avoid the challenges and your passion deflates even more.

But this also works in reverse. Passion is the inner drive that can take an impossible situation and turn it into a possible situation. People who have passion do not see impossible circumstances; they see opportunities. Passion will always ignite creativity, allowing you to find solutions. Therefore, you invest in opportunities when you fire up your passion.

You invest in opportunities when you prepare yourself for them. Preparation will always recognize opportunity because preparation causes you to live life in expectation and diligently position yourself for the coming window of opportunity. A person can become intellectually and mentally fit to face challenges and opposing points of view. A person who is not prepared to meet opportunities will see them passing by without having the possibility of seizing them.

As I mentioned when I discussed time, one of the things you have to understand in this context is that *preparation is never wasted time.* History always repeats itself, and throughout the ages, basic human needs have not changed, only the form in which they manifest. If you want to look for answers about the future, you don't need a crystal ball; all you have to do is to study the patterns of the past. Winston Churchill once said, "The farther back you can look, the farther forward you are likely to see." Preparation will position you ahead of the curve and you will be there, positioned and ready, when the events happen.

You invest in opportunities when you provide solutions to problems. As you have seen, the *problem vs. solution* topic has come up several times in this book. This is because of its complexity and because it affects many of the concepts described. Still, every time we bring it up, we are analyzing a new facet. Facing a *problem* would cause you to flip it around and look for the *opportunity* behind it. This is the time to start thinking and working in order to push out a *solution.*

All successful people are people who seize the moment. When you blame circumstances for your own failure, you devalue yourself. The same circumstance can be a problem or an opportunity, but you either choose to see it as an obstacle, something that sets you back, or a chance, something you can use as a trampoline toward the future. The most common mistake is to look for a solution outside the problem when, in most cases, the solution is baked into the problem.

We mentioned in the beginning of this chapter that we often do not see opportunities if they come in "working clothes." We are looking for that great "aha" idea that will make us multimillionaires overnight, but we are not so willing to make the effort required to make it a reality. Taking advantage of an opportunity means to seize it, exploit it, satisfy its need, create value, and watch it work toward our own prosperity. This also requires looking for a cure that eliminates the cause of the problem, not just addresses the symptoms. Too often, we look at the effects and find remedies that wipe them out without addressing the root cause. This will prove to be a temporary solution because, if the root cause is still present, the symptoms will sooner or later show up again. They may be in the same or a different form, but they will definitely show up.

You invest in opportunities when you stay focused on the future. I have mentioned before that *lost focus* is one of the root causes of failure. You may identify an opportunity; you may even start pursuing it and then build on it, devoting lots of effort, but the only way to reap the results of those efforts is to stay focused until the end.

Some years ago, I was in charge of developing a catering and restaurant business in Romania. In a country and a time of full development after the collapse of Communism, it was possible to grow, in only five years, a small business (eight employees and roughly $50,000 in annual turnover) into a medium-size enterprise with over 200 employees and over $2.5 million in sales. It was a huge opportunity, both in the business market (as multinational corporations were marching into the country) and retail market (as restaurant patrons became more sophisticated and demanded quality services). Our growth was so successful that the company became a candidate for being acquired by a huge multinational corporation, in a proposed multimillion-dollar transaction.

What went wrong? Unfortunately, due to disagreements between shareholders, I allowed myself to lose focus on the future of the company—something that was, for me, a painful experience and a hard-learned lesson. Instead of concentrating my efforts on the future of the business, I was more concerned about making the point that without my personal involvement, the company was not worth too much. I was right. After I left the company, the multinational corporation withdrew their offer, and due to lack of vision, it took just a short time before the entire company was history. Our restaurants and coffee shops were closed one after another, employees were sent home, and all shareholders lost everything. I understood later on that it was a high price to pay for me proving a point. Five years of hard work were wasted. But the hard lesson learned was that whenever you identify and pursue an *opportunity*, you have to stay focused on the future in order to make it an *investment*.

You invest in opportunities when you fight rejection. I mentioned already that opportunities stand by silently and wait to be recognized. Sometimes, we recognize them and are willing to act upon them. But things may not be as obvious for others as they are for us, and consequently, people will reject our ideas, products, or services. Fighting and resisting that rejection is a way to invest in that opportunity. John Paul DeJoria, billionaire and philanthropist, best known as cofounder of the John Paul Mitchell Systems, explained in his conference held in 2011 at Stanford Graduate School of Business,

> Be prepared for a lot of rejection. I do not care how good your idea is, if you are not prepared for it in advance, you will be tempted to believe that it may not be a good idea, because fifty people said no. When you knock on door no.

51, you have to be as enthusiastic as when you knocked on the first door—even if the first fifty doors were slammed in your face. (*www.youtube.com/watch?v=hndfUwPpzyQ*)

You invest in opportunities when you carefully evaluate all the risks. I have already said that we invest in opportunities when we prepare ourselves for them. This means that we also learn as much as possible about the opportunity area we want to take advantage of. No area of investment, not even government bonds, can any longer be considered risk free (or 100 percent safe). Accumulating knowledge in the particular area in which you want to invest will significantly reduce the risk of making a bad decision, and subsequently, you will make fewer and fewer bad decisions.

You need to understand the potential pitfalls—to be aware of what might go wrong and plan actions that reduce the probability of occurrence of the unwanted events. Further, you need to evaluate and understand the impact of an event because, if the event occurs despite your efforts to avoid it, you have to be prepared to limit the impact of that event.

You invest in opportunities when developing healthy relationships based on trust. I discussed this topic when I said that time dedicated to developing healthy relationships is *invested time*. But relationships are not only about time. Good relationships represent one of the best environments to ensure a continuous flow of opportunities. One of the key elements in a relationship is *trust*, and trust is one of the most important personal assets. Being trustworthy will open many doors because people always prefer to deal with a reliable, trustworthy person. Whether we are talking about investments, partnerships, or just job openings, people will appreciate working with somebody they trust. This will also increase the chances of getting positive answers when you ask for favors. The flip side of the story is also true. While trust represents an asset, *lack of trust* can be seen as a major *liability*. People avoid dealing with you and you lose opportunities for referrals of any sort.

Conclusions

In this book, I have tried to make the case that wealth is everywhere, all around us. In addition to explaining why I believe this, I made references to people who are living proof of this concept. Everyone who has been quoted in this book is a person who will always be remembered for the legacy they leave behind. And, of course, all of them were (or are) wealthy, despite the fact that they started barehanded and they managed to build their wealth against all odds. In this final section, I would like to summarize some of the main ideas.

Wealth is not about ownership, but rather about access and possession. Ownership can distort the way you look at material things, and this is why I claim that possessing allows you to increase. Your spirit of survival and self-preservation will tempt you into hoarding and will make it difficult for you to let go of some things. Further, this limits your availability to trade up the things you own, even though the trade would clearly be in your advantage. This is why I claim that wealth is about access and possession rather than ownership. This does not mean you have to give away anything. The things will continue to be formally registered in your name; it is just a matter of how you perceive them. Everything you possess has value as long as somebody else accepts that value. The potential buyer decides the value. By the way, this is why personal things with emotional value are not valued highly. This also applies to currency (which is in fact the thing we call "money")—which is just an image of perceived value. If somebody else does not believe it's money, then the value diminishes.

I also claimed that wealth is not about having a lot of money, but about having abundance of assets. An asset, by definition, is something that produces income. Wealth grows when we are in possession of income-producing assets. Tangible goods that you *possess* (e.g., cars, furniture, decorations) may make you feel like you "own assets," but they are not really producing any form of revenue. They are in fact consumables, because they depreciate until you eventually replace them after some years, but since you can use them for a longer time, you treat them like assets. Everything that takes money out of your pocket for use or maintenance is a *liability*.

Through my research, I found out that *every person on this planet is given four resources: creativity (which means gifts and talents), time, knowledge (which means information, knowledge, and wisdom), and opportunities.* You can build wealth by investing these resources—this means that you release them with the purpose of generating a flow of future benefits. These benefits can be in monetary terms and can be used to purchase more income-producing assets or even consumable possessions that make your life better. But the benefits are not limited to money; they can provide access to new resources that you were not given access to in the first place. Also, you can spend these resources; this means to get something else in return that can be used for investment. For sure, you have to avoid wasting them—meaning you release them without any form of future benefits and you don't get anything in exchange. This is the worst part, and always leads to poverty. Therefore, you have to understand that there is a thin line between spending and wasting. Many times you believe you are spending, but in fact you are wasting—because what you get in return is just consumable goods that will very soon depreciate.

As long as wealth can be built using these resources available to everybody, there is another conclusion to be drawn—*that you are not entitled to anything in this world*. Mark Twain made a very clear point: "Don't go around saying the world owes you a living. The world owes you nothing. It was here first." An entitlement mentality is a major killer to building wealth. Nobody owes you anything just because you simply showed up on planet Earth. Indeed, parents have a responsibility to feed and clothe their children and also to guide them in life. Surely, not all parents excel in that; in fact, some do a very poor job. But later on, when you become an adult and are able to make your own choices, you are the only one responsible and in charge of your life. Nobody is entitled to a trouble-free and prosperous life. You may inherit such, as part of your blessings, but you are not entitled to it. Politicians and governments like to offer this, but their promises, like any other promises people make, are always conditional.

It is up to you to make sure you do not take the bait into this entitlement mentality. The more you distance yourself from it, the more successful you will become. This is because entitlement focuses on your weaknesses—"I deserve it because I cannot get it myself, and somebody else, who is stronger than me, should deliver." On the other hand, when you distance yourself from entitlement, you focus on your inner strengths—making it possible to make life better, not only for you, but also for the ones around you. One of the best statements that support this can be found in Steve Forbes's book *A New Birth of Freedom*, where he concluded,

> The real source of wealth and capital in this new era is not material things—it is the human mind, the human spirit, the human imagination and our faith in the future. That's the magic of a free society—everyone can move forward and prosper because wealth comes from within.

As I pointed out in the Introduction, most people are looking for a magic formula that grows their little money geometrically. They want to find that safe investment vehicle where they can invest just a few dollars that turns into a thousand times more in a short time. In this book, I did not try to prove that this formula doesn't exist. It may very well exist. But the wealthy people I examined did not have a magic formula for overnight miracle wealth building. It was, and still is, their personal choices, responsibility, and use of the four resources—*creativity, time, knowledge,* and *opportunities*—that made the entire difference between their becoming a *wealth maker* and not remaining a *wishful thinker.*

About the Author

Iustin Rosioara is an experienced professional in several industries and service areas. His career spans three decades and many professions, including industrial plant development, automation processes, construction management, real estate development, real estate management, retail, and hospitality.

With a Master of Science degree in Electronic Engineering from the University of Bucharest (Romania) and Norges Tekniske Hoyskole in Trondheim (Norway), Iustin Rosioara holds certifications in the areas of Project Management, Property Management, Computer Systems Engineering and Service Quality.

Find more at *www.MasteringTheHumanExperience.com*

<u>Published books:</u>

Threaded Property Exchange: Streamlining the Process of Selling and Buying Residential Properties. Published in Bucharest, Romania, 2012

> The *Threaded Property Exchange Method* is a way to streamline the process of selling and buying residential properties. Regardless of whether the market is low or high, most buyers and sellers are looking for an exchange. Most people want to sell because they are in the process of buying something else. The *Threaded Property Exchange Method* provides a low risk and virtually seamless transaction flow paradigm for buying and selling residential properties.

Common Sense Answers to Everyday Questions: Money, Currency and Credit. Published by Service Strategy Solutions LLC, St. Paul, MN, US, 2015.

In the era of *"credit*-ism," some people see everything related to money as a conspiracy of the elite vs. the masses, while others claim that our financial world has become so complex that only specialists can understand it. Consequently, it is important for each of us to understand what is really happening and the factors that affect and influence our own lives. *Common Sense Answers to Everyday Questions: Money, Currency and Credit*, explores the true nature of money and currencies and the constant need for credit in our modern society. It provides an important first step in establishing true financial freedom.

Common Sense Answers to Everyday Questions: Inflation and Deflation. Published by Service Strategy Solutions LLC, St. Paul, MN, US, 2015.

How do we, by adjusting our spending patterns due to changes in our environment, unknowingly participate in the processes of inflation and deflation? *Common Sense Answers to Everyday Questions: Inflation and Deflation*, answers these questions by delving into the processes that cause inflation and deflation as perceived by the individual. It looks beyond the technical aspects of money printing or credit destruction and explores the psychological aspects that directly and indirectly affect price increases or decreases.